CRITICAL
ANTHOLOGIES OF
NONFICTION
WRITING ™

CRITICAL PERSPECTIVES ON GENETICALLY MODIFIED CROPS AND FOOD

Edited by
Susan Gordon

631.5233
CRI

THE ROSEN PUBLISHING GROUP, INC.
NEW YORK

Published in 2006 by The Rosen Publishing Group, Inc.
29 East 21st Street, New York, NY 10010

Copyright © 2006 by The Rosen Publishing Group, Inc.

First Edition

Library of Congress Cataloging-in-Publication Data

Critical perspectives on genetically modified crops and food/ edited by Susan Gordon.—1st ed.
    p. cm.
Includes bibliographical references and index.
ISBN 1-4042-0541-1 (lib. bdg.)
1. Transgenic plants. 2. Crops—Genetic engineering. 3. Genetically modified foods.
I. Gordon, Susan.
SB123.57.C75 2006
631.5'233—dc22

                                                        2005012848

Manufactured in the United States of America

On the cover: A field of ripening corn.

CONTENTS

Introduction   **5**

CHAPTER ONE

Time, Continuity, and Change: THE EVOLUTION OF GM CROPS   **9**

From *Travels in the Genetically Modified Zone*
   by Mark L. Winston   10
From *Mendel in the Kitchen* by Nina Fedoroff
   and Nancy Marie Brown   21
From *DNA* by James D. Watson   32
From "Billions Served" by Ronald Bailey   44

CHAPTER TWO

Science, Technology, and Society: FOOD FOR EARTH   **52**

From *Food, Inc.* by Peter Pringle   53
"A Cure for the Common Farm?" by Lucinda Fleeson   63
"Grains of Hope" by J. Madeleine Nash   68

CHAPTER THREE

Production, Distribution, and Consumption:
   THE IMPACT OF GM FOODS   **81**

"The World in a Seed" by John Feffer   82
"Facing Biotech Foods Without the Fear Factor"
   by Jane E. Brody   89
From *The Botany of Desire* by Michael Pollan   94

CHAPTER FOUR

Power, Authority, and Governance: FOOD AND LAW   **105**

From "Agricultural Biotechnology"
   by Michael F. Jacobson   106
From *Eating in the Dark* by Kathleen Hart   118
From *Dinner at the New Gene Café* by Bill Lambrecht   130
From *Lords of the Harvest* by Daniel Charles   137

CHAPTER FIVE Global Connections: WHAT THE WORLD WANTS FOR DINNER **144**
"Consumers in Europe Resist Gene-Altered Foods"
   by Lizette Alvarez 145
"Argentina's Bitter Harvest" by Sue Branford 150
"Far Less Scary Than It Used to Be" by the *Economist* 159

Timeline **168**
For More Information **171**
For Further Reading **172**
Annotated Bibliography **174**
Index **178**

INTRODUCTION

Humans have been selectively breeding and manipulating food crops for ages, but the ability to alter the genes of an organism in the laboratory was only first realized in 1953. That year, at Cambridge University in England, James Watson and Francis Crick discovered the structure of deoxyribonucleic acid, or DNA, the basic building block of life. This discovery galvanized the scientific community, which saw in DNA the potential for revolutionary advances in biology and medicine. At the same time, the discovery also created new yearnings in the business community, which saw new technologies with great potential for profit.

In January 1983, a scientist named Rob Horsch gave a brief talk about his work with genetically engineered seeds at a biotechnology conference in Miami, Florida. Horsch's presentation marked the entry of the Monsanto Corporation into the field of genetically modified (GM) foods. This field had previously been the domain of independent scientists, but now the future of the science was in the hands of a large, corporate institution. Almost overnight, Monsanto became the leader of the industry. In the next two decades, scientists at Monsanto would dramatically change the nature of farming and food production.

Monsanto's influence, and the influence of similar corporations, remain at the heart of the GM foods debate. Can corporations be trusted to make decisions about what is safe for us to eat? The articles in this anthology will address this question, along with many others.

The science behind GM crops and food is not overly complex. When the genes of an organism such as a plant or a bacterium are restructured in the lab, the organism is said to be genetically modified. The process is known as genetic engineering. Genetic engineering generally involves removing portions of DNA from a donor organism, "splicing" them into the genetic material of a virus, and then introducing that virus into a host organism. The host organism incorporates the new DNA and then begins to express it. Usually, this new DNA changes only one trait of the organism. For example, a genetically engineered plant might produce vitamin A, while the non-GM plant would not. In the 1980s, Monsanto and a few similar companies began to concentrate on developing genetic technology that could be used to make new breeds of crops. By 1994, the first genetically modified food reached the supermarket shelves.

Today, opinions concerning GM foods vary widely. Those in favor of genetically modified plants insist that the greater crop yields and nutrition they provide will counter high farming costs and low food supplies throughout the world. Yet there are also many people who say that genetically engineered crops are dangerous to the environment, to the economy, and to human health.

Many environmentalists worry about the lack of research on long-term environmental effects of farming GM crops. They are concerned that genetically modified organisms (GMOs) will cross-pollinate and alter non-GM crops, creating uncontrollable and irreversible conditions within nature. Another concern is that some crops are engineered so that they are not damaged by herbicides, allowing farmers to use large amounts of these chemicals to destroy weeds. The herbicides, however, leave lasting toxins in the environment and may cause illnesses in humans. Despite this, government agencies and agribusiness corporations tell consumers that genetic engineering can be controlled and can create safe products.

Economic concerns have been raised as well. Over the past two decades, many genetically modified crops have been created to increase food production while lowering farming costs. Some genetically engineered plants can create their own pesticides, saving farmers money and time. However, critics point out that the high costs of seeds, fertilizers, and irrigation systems needed to grow GM crops outweigh any potential savings for small, family-owned farms. The large sums of money needed to grow GM crops, critics contend, transform farming into a business controlled by a small number of large producers. In order to keep up with the high start-up costs, small farmers often must take out large loans. In addition, the concept of seed ownership fuels bitter debates. If farmers are only allowed to plant the seeds they buy from GM seed companies such as Monsanto, they will lose even more power to those companies.

Regulation is yet another issue that is far more complex than it may appear at first glance. Consumers, particularly in European countries, remain highly suspicious of genetically engineered foods. Some countries have required that imported foods receive labels describing their genetic makeup. The effects of eating food containing GM ingredients are unclear and still hotly debated. In part, this is because not enough time has passed to study the long-term effects. At the time of this writing, GMOs have made their way into 60 to 70 percent of the food sold in supermarkets across the United States. U.S. consumer advocates raise several questions: Should food that contains GMOs be labeled so that consumers know what they are about to eat? And, if so, is it enough to list the genetically modified ingredients, or do labels need to also make clear exactly how these ingredients have been modified?

The questions concerning GM foods remain thorny and the answers difficult to discern. The selections you are about to read will give you an overview of the many issues that have come to light since Rob Horsch stood up to talk about his work at Monsanto fewer than three short decades ago. —*SG*

CHAPTER ONE

TIME, CONTINUITY, AND CHANGE: THE EVOLUTION OF GM CROPS

To some degree, farming has always involved genetic manipulation. Early agriculture was largely about identifying and planting the seeds that would result in high-yield crops or crops with desirable traits. These practices carried on for centuries, creating more and more genetically specialized crops. Then came the green revolution, a period that began roughly in the 1960s, and resulted in huge increases in crop yields.

Initially, experimentation during the green revolution occurred through relatively natural means. Today's strategies of genetic manipulation began in the 1970s and exploded in the 1990s, when the U.S. government reduced safety regulations. The results have yielded promises of an end to world starvation but also widespread fears of superbugs and other negative side effects of genetically modified crops.

In the following excerpt from his book Travels in the Genetically Modified Zone, *Mark L. Winston provides a summary of important events that led to GM crops, from the domestication of crops 10,000 years ago, to the scientific discoveries of Gregor Mendel, to the business strategies of an entrepreneur from Iowa named Roswell Garst.* —SG

From *Travels in the Genetically Modified Zone*
by Mark L. Winston
2002

A seed is a marvelous entity, expressing a tiny moment of evolutionary history. Its ancestors evolved through billions of years, beginning with the most primitive bacteria, evolving on past the earliest plantlike organisms to the seeds of contemporary and complex plants. Soon it will fall to the ground and sprout, producing its own offspring, which will continue the evolutionary dance through endless years of future birth and death, its descendants' traits mediated by the ongoing forge of natural selection.

Evolution and natural selection are without purpose or goal, but they have inexorably increased biodiversity. First kingdoms, then phyla, and on through species, the numbers and types of organisms have grown steadily over time. Occasionally there has been a catastrophe of epic scope that diminished diversity to a shadow of its former exuberance—a meteor hitting the earth, a volcano darkening the globe, tectonic shifts submerging continents. Inevitably the biological world rebounded, with new groups of species slowly diversifying until the next natural disaster.

Now we have imposed a new twist—biotechnology—on this pattern of fluctuating diversity. Today we are selectively, deliberately, and surgically reinventing the plant world, rearranging genomes in a matter of months or years, at rates astronomically faster than natural selection itself or even traditional plant breeding could produce new varieties.

Contemporary seeds are increasingly designed by humans, with implications of the profoundest magnitude for both agriculture and what remains of the wild world.

Our current ability to precisely engineer crop genomes was preceded by a long history of genetic manipulation in agriculture. Human impact and its accompanying effects began early in our history, at many tropical and subtropical sites around the globe. Our ancestors were omnivores, fortuitously consuming whatever plant or animal material they encountered. Even then humans had considerable effects on the environment, reducing and even driving to extinction populations of the animal species they hunted and expanding the distribution of plants by accidentally distributing seeds as they migrated.

Humans probably first realized that seeds could yield a stable food supply through agriculture when they observed plants arising from refuse or wasteland, perhaps fruit trees growing along forest and jungle paths from discarded or defecated seeds, or vegetables sprouting in garbage dumps at temporary settlements. A more organized approach to agriculture began about eight to ten thousand years ago, coincidentally at a number of locations around the globe. The most diverse farming developed in the Near East, with legumes, cereals, flax, sesame, and fruit trees. At about the same time, New World residents were growing beans, maize, squashes, and potatoes, and Asian farmers were beginning to cultivate rice.

These early domesticated crops foreshadowed the overwhelming changes contemporary agriculture has wrought in plants. Humans soon learned to separate crop varieties from wild types, in order to prevent characteristics undesirable for cultivation from mingling with those selected for farming. Continued selection of crops with desirable characteristics increased the separation between feral and managed plants, and accelerated the diminishing diversity and more limited variation found in today's crops.

The simplest way to select crops is to save seeds preferentially from plants with beneficial traits, and the first farmers selected for large seeds and fruit, increased seed production, lack of dormancy, faster germination, higher annual yield, and reduced seed scattering. The success of this early selection resulted in an accelerating impact of agriculture on crop diversity and feral plants. Crops quickly became commodities, moved and traded over a rapidly widening area, so that many plants were distributed well beyond their previous ranges, and some throughout the globe.

Three phenomena have characterized the more recent impact of agriculture on the earth. The first was the increase in human population, which has doubled at shorter and shorter intervals over the last thousand years. The result was increased acreage under cultivation and a fundamental remodeling of the globe toward managed rather than wild ecosystems. By 1998, 3,410,523,800 acres of land were under cultivation worldwide, an area larger than the United States. Entire ecosystems have disappeared, others remain but are threatened, and the sheer volume of people and area of farmland has been a major force of biological change.

The second event through which agriculture modified our planet was European colonization. Previously, migration and trade had moved crops between countries and continents, but the Europeans inaugurated an unprecedented dispersal of biological material worldwide. Corn, tomatoes, and potatoes were transported from the New World to the Old; wheat, rye, and barley carried from the Old World to the New; and rice, soybeans, and alfalfa moved from their Asian sources to every arable continent. Each of these and innumerable other introductions conveyed not only unique genetic material, but also assemblages of introduced plant pests and diseases that today cause the majority of pest-management problems around the world.

The third factor shaping the nature of agriculture and the environment alike is the increasing precision with which we have selected and bred crops. This acuity stemmed from many advances, but at its heart lies the work of two men, one the English naturalist Charles Darwin and the other an Austrian monk, Gregor Mendel. The concepts of evolution and genetics were not their work alone, but both of them were decades ahead of their colleagues in synthesizing the companion concepts of natural selection and inheritance that are at the core of all contemporary biological science, and that form the substrate upon which biotechnology grew.

In retrospect, it is remarkable how dramatically our farmer ancestors changed crop plants through selecting desirable varieties, given how little they knew about natural selection and heredity. We now know much more about the concepts underlying variation, and particularly about the extent to which many plants can recombine their genetic material and absorb genes from related species. Critics of genetically modified crops may find it uncomfortable to contemplate, but plants are naturally fluid in their propensity to blend genomes. Our ability to mix and match genetically controlled traits artificially had become extensive even before Darwin and Mendel, but the twin pillars of evolution and genetics accelerated advances in horticulture and led to unprecedented advances in varietal selection and breeding.

Darwin's impact was felt first. Although we remember him primarily for his role in expressing the concepts of evolution and natural selection, his work also had a transforming impact on crop breeding. Indeed, he began *The Origin of Species* with a chapter titled "Variation under Domestication," reflecting the considerable influence that crop, pet, and livestock breeding had on his thinking. Darwin noted that plants show extensive variation in nature, and suggested that much of this expressed variability is pruned out by natural selection. Farmers, however, can propagate and nurture desirable traits that might not survive in the wild but can thrive under cultivation.

Domestication demonstrated for Darwin the inherent simplicity of choosing successive generations of gradually improving stock that over time could transform inferior plants into functional crops: "No one would expect to raise a first-rate melting pear from the seed of the wild pear . . . The pear, though cultivated in classical times, appears from Pliny's description to have been a fruit of very inferior quality. I have seen great surprise expressed in horticultural works at the wonderful skill of gardeners, in having produced such splendid results from such poor materials . . . The gardeners of the classical period, who cultivated the best pear they could procure, never thought what splendid fruit we should eat, though we owe our excellent fruit . . . to their having naturally chosen and preserved the best varieties they could anywhere find."

Crop selection had been operating under Darwinian principles for millennia, but it was Darwin's articulation of the inherent and extensive variation within species, the nature of heredity; and the similarities between artificial and natural selection that provided a clear explanation for what farmers had been doing intuitively since the beginning of agriculture. Perhaps the most remarkable aspect of Darwin's theories was that he was not aware of the physical mechanisms of genetics responsible for determining heredity. As he put it, "The laws governing inheritance are quite unknown," and although the key breakthrough was published in 1866, the laws of heredity were to continue languishing in obscurity until the early 1900s.

Gregor Mendel added the second insight leading to scientific plant breeding and eventually biotechnology with his research demonstrating the particulate nature of inheritance. He, too, was missing an important part of the puzzle, since the composition of the "particles" was not fully explained until the second half of the twentieth century. Nevertheless, his careful breeding experiments with peas provided the framework upon which the science of modern genetics grew.

Mendel was the son of an Austrian farmer, ordained as a priest in 1847 and later made abbot at the Augustinian monastery in Brünn, Austria-Hungary. Although he taught science, Mendel was a poor student, and never passed his formal examinations in spite of many years of his own remedial schooling. He worked alone, spending close to ten years crossing peas and observing generations of offspring.

Mendel examined many traits, including the easily visible characteristics of seed shape, plant height, and floral color, and noted that traits seemed to skip a generation in being expressed when plants of different types were crossed. He calculated the mathematics of the inheritance patterns he observed, and determined that each trait was dominant or recessive, inherited independently, half from the father and half from the mother plant. These concepts inevitably led to the conclusion that heredity involved physical particles, which we now know as genes and the chromosomes that carry them.

Mendel's work was published in scientific journals, and presented at a number of meetings, but oddly was lost to mainstream science until 1900, when three other European botanists independently arrived at the same results when experimenting with other plant systems. All three rediscovered and cited Mendel's work when searching the literature before publishing their own research, and thus he justly received credit for discovering the physical nature of heredity.

Scientists soon understood that heredity was determined by particles within cells, and that chromosomes composed of DNA carried these particles, or genes. At this point all the components were in place for contemporary approaches to plant breeding, including an understanding of evolution, selection, and the nature of inheritance, as well as the ability to predict results from designated crosses between varieties. With these conceptual and practical tools, plant breeders made enormous strides in developing new crop varieties . . .

Genetically modified crops would not have been successful in 1930 even had the methodology been available, because agribusiness infrastructure and farming practices were not yet ready for biotechnology. Roswell Garst made immense contributions to the agriculture of his time, and his life's work was a necessary precursor to transgenic crops in our time. He and his compatriots changed the lifestyle of agriculture: they transformed individual self-reliant farmers into a community of growers highly dependent on multifaceted companies that supported high-input agriculture, thereby providing a corporate template through which genetically modified crops could enter the marketplace.

Garst persuaded farmers to stop saving seeds every year and instead to purchase their seeds from companies that had selected more productive varieties, creating a dependency on seeds produced by corporations, new crop varieties to which genes eventually would be transferred, and a sales network through which genetically modified seeds would be sold to farmers in our generation. American farmers also began producing excess food as a result of Garst's influence, and this surplus combined with increased input costs created an economic environment that is driving agriculture toward biotechnological solutions to the problem of a collapsing farm economy. Garst also made international trade arrangements with developing countries that today remain as possible conduits for genetically modified crops. Finally, he was confident that agricultural problems could be solved, an attitude that in many ways was his most important legacy to what eventually became agricultural biotechnology.

Garst grew up in a farming community, and given his background, enterprising nature, and intuitive feeling for agriculture, it is not surprising that he had become a successful dairy farmer by the 1920s. He was restless, however, and when his father died and subsequently the family's general store was sold, Garst moved to Des Moines, Iowa, to subdivide and sell 120 acres of former farmland at the city limits.

Garst and his new wife, Elizabeth, were well connected to Des Moines society through their family's long history as successful merchants and farmers. They soon began moving in the same circles as Henry A. Wallace, who was from a highly distinguished third-generation Iowa family and would later become U.S. Secretary of Agriculture under Franklin D. Roosevelt and eventually make an unsuccessful run for the Presidency. Wallace was then editor of *Wallace's Farmer*, the most influential farm newspaper in the Midwest, and on the side he had developed a serious interest in corn breeding.

Wallace perfected techniques to produce the higher-yielding hybrid corns by detasseling male plants and thereby preventing undesired crosses. Corn has its male pollen-producing structures located in the tassels at the top of the plant, and the female part that produces the ears of corn is located farther down on the stalk. Wallace would cut off the tassels of one variety planted next to a row of a second variety, on which he would leave the pollen-producing tassels intact. This procedure insured that pollination would occur only between the tasseled variety and the other detasseled line, resulting in outcrossing between inbred varieties and the higher-yielding hybridized corn.

Garst quickly grasped the sales potential of these superior-yielding varieties, and offered to sell Wallace's hybrid corn to farmers as seed corn from which to grow their crops. The arrangement they made was that Wallace's new company Pioneer Hi-Bred, would select and breed the inbred lines, and provide those to Garst under license; then Garst's new company

Garst Seeds, would plant this foundation stock in sufficient quantities to produce enough hybrid seed corn for farmers to purchase the following season.

By 1930 the Great Depression had hit, Garst's Des Moines subdivision was moribund, and he and Elizabeth had moved back to the family farm in Coon Rapids. At the time corn farmers were not accustomed to buying seed, or in fact to buying almost anything. Typically Iowa farmers purchased only salt and nails, and were otherwise self-contained, saving part of their crop for next year's seed, using manure for fertilizer, and relying on draft horses to plow in the spring and pull trailers in the late summer, into which they threw the hand-picked and husked corn they harvested.

Selling seed corn to this clientele would have been tough at any time, but during the Depression it seemed an impossible task. Garst hit on an ingenious strategy giving farmers free bags of corn in the spring and asking only that they pay him half of the increased yield from his hybrid corn in the fall. When his superior varieties out-performed the farmers' seeds, Garst accepted only the cost of the seed corn he had given the farmers in the spring, along with their commitment to buy seeds from him the following season. He also created a sales network, with the most respected farmers in each county across the Midwest as his representatives. Within a decade most farmers had switched to buying seed with cash.

The same sort of thing happened with many contemporary crops: a few varieties are selected by experts, maintained by corporations, and sold to farmers. Hybrid corn is clearly more productive, but farmers cannot maintain these lines themselves. The parent inbred lines are too complex to produce and maintain without considerable scientific input and an elaborate breeding program. Further, hybrid corn is genetically handicapped by a diminished ability to grow viable, productive plants in future generations, so that saving hybrid seed is not sensible.

As a result, corn farmers ceased selecting and saving their own seeds and came to depend on newly developing corporations such as Garst Seeds that specialized in hybrid seed corn production. This system was integral in improving productivity but it also changed farming from a simple occupation to an industry and severely reduced the number of varieties being produced for commercial agriculture. In the United States, for example, 786 corn varieties were available in 1903, but only 52 in 1983, a decrease of 93 percent. Thus farmers who became used to purchasing the latest hybrid variety from their favored seed company each spring were ideally predisposed to accept transgenic corn when those varieties became the corn of choice recommended by seed companies in the mid-1990s.

Not only did farmers become dependent on agricultural conglomerates for seed to plant each season, but they came to rely on those companies for an increasingly essential array of pesticides to combat pests, weeds, and diseases, synthetic fertilizer to reach the yield potential contained within hybrid seeds, and increasingly specialized and sophisticated farm machinery to harvest the more uniform corn plants that lent themselves to mechanical picking and processing. Garst invested in all these areas, inventing new machinery and promoting the benefits of heavy synthetic fertilizer applications that interacted with hybrid corn to further boost production.

Agribusiness had been born, integrating seeds, fertilizers, pesticides, and farm machinery into a corporate structure, with suppliers linked by increasingly complex business relationships.

———■———

An organism that has received genetic material from a differ-ent species is called a chimera, named after a mythical beast that possessed the features of a lion, a serpent, and a goat. Genetically engineered seeds or plants are chimeras that have been designed to fulfill a specific purpose—often to increase crop yields or nutritional value. The science behind these botanical chimeras has been more than fifty years in the mak-ing, beginning with Watson and Crick's discovery of the structure of DNA in 1953, and continuing to today's scien-tists who seek more efficient and effective ways to introduce foreign genes into plants.

In the following excerpt from their book Mendel in the Kitchen, *Nina Fedoroff and Nancy Marie Brown take a his-torical look at the work of three scientific teams, each of which has made significant contributions to our ability to create chimeras in the laboratory.* —SG

From *Mendel in the Kitchen: A Scientist's View of Genetically Modified Foods*
by Nina Fedoroff and Nancy Marie Brown
2004

Stanley Cohen and Herbert Boyer were familiar with the botan-ical use of the term chimera when they began the collaboration that would result in their chimeric DNA molecules, ones in which DNA from two different species were spliced together. The technique they developed—at about the same time as Downey and Stefansson developed canola—is the essence of recombinant DNA technology. It makes the modern genetic modification of food plants possible.

Cohen at Stanford University was interested in plasmids, the tiny circular extra chromosomes in bacteria. He had been studying plasmids that carry drug-resistance genes since he arrived at Stanford in 1968; by then 60 to 80 percent of bacteria were showing resistance to more than one antibiotic drug. Cohen hoped to learn how bacteria used plasmids to pass around their resistance genes so that the process could be slowed or stopped. "One of the goals of my research," he said in a 1992 lecture, "was to map and characterize plasmid genes. To do this I wanted to be able to take plasmids apart and put them back together again one segment at a time."

In 1971, Leslie Shiyu, a first-year Stanford medical student working in Cohen's lab, discovered that when bacteria were treated with the chemical calcium chloride, they took up plasmids, replicated them, and passed them on to their progeny. Cohen reported these results at a conference in Hawaii. "Later that day I listened with excitement," he recalls, as Herbert Boyer, then at the University of California at San Francisco (UCSF), described experiments in his lab using enzymes to cut apart and glue back together segments of DNA. "That evening," Cohen recalls, "Herb and I, joined by several other friends and colleagues, had a late night snack at a delicatessen across from Waikiki Beach." Over hot pastrami and corned beef sandwiches Cohen proposed a collaboration.

The experiment involved two plasmids from Cohen's lab: one plasmid conferred resistance to the antibiotic tetracycline; another, larger plasmid carried resistance to the antibiotic kanamycin. The experiment also required two enzymes, isolated in Boyer's lab. One, called *EcoRI*, was a restriction endonuclease; like molecular scissors, it could cut the plasmid DNA apart. The various cut fragments could be glued back together with the second enzyme, called a ligase. The tetracycline-resistant plasmid would be cut open, offered the piece of the other plasmid that contained the kanamycin-resistance gene, and glued shut. The recombined, or recombinant, plasmid would then be introduced into bacteria, and they would be exposed to the two antibiotics. If the bacteria lived, it meant that the tetracycline-resistant plasmid had picked up and copied, or cloned, the fragment of DNA containing the kanamycin-resistance gene.

Cohen recalls: "The months in early 1973 were a period of almost unbelievable excitement. The strategy worked even better than we could have expected and on most days there was a new result and a new high. Plasmids were isolated at Stanford, transported to UCSF where they were cut by *EcoRI* and analyzed, and then transferred back to Stanford where the DNA fragments were joined and the plasmids were reintroduced into bacteria." Annie Chang, a research technician in Cohen's laboratory, isolated the plasmid DNA and introduced it into the bacteria. Soon the team was joined by John Morrow of Stanford and Howard Goodman in UCSF in an effort to clone animal (in this case, toad) genes instead of bacterial genes in a plasmid. That strategy worked too, as did one that Cohen and Chang, working with Stanford's Robert Schimke, devised a few years later: they inserted a mouse gene into *E. coli* and showed that the bacterium could express the protein the mouse gene coded for.

They called their recombinant DNA molecules chimeras, Cohen wrote, "because they were conceptually similar to the mythological Chimera . . . and were the molecular counterparts of hybrid plant chimeras produced by agricultural grafting." . . .

The Cohen-Boyer experiments were a milestone because they showed that DNA could be recombined in a test tube. They were not, however, the first time a bacterial cell had been genetically engineered.

In the early 1950s Norton Zinder, then a graduate student in the laboratory of Joshua Lederberg at the University of Wisconsin, showed that viruses could move genes from one bacterial genome into another. As a graduate student himself in the late 1940s Lederberg had discovered sex in bacteria. Until then it was thought that rather than mating and mingling the genes of father and mother a bacterium simply doubled its own genes and split into two genetically identical daughter cells: they were clones. In animals, only identical twins are clones. But plants commonly clone themselves in nature by such devices as underground runners. Stands of poplar, for example, are all clones. And cloning is commonly used to propagate food crops. Potatoes grown from potato eyes are clones, as are raspberry shoots raised from suckers, or apples from grafted branches. Indeed, the word "clone" comes from the art of grafting: it is Greek for "twig."

Lederberg found that bacteria were not all clones. Bacteria have a single circular chromosome consisting of several thousand genes. But most bacterial cells also contain those tiny circles of DNA called plasmids, a name Lederberg coined. Although they replicate at the same time as the bacterium's own chromosome, these plasmids generally remain separate, pursuing their own independent lifestyle. Some plasmids very occasionally integrate themselves into the bacterial chromosome, melding the two into one larger circle. And, as Lederberg discovered, plasmids often carry genes that tell the bacterium to create a connection—a tube or bridge—to another bacterium, through which the plasmid transfers itself. If the plasmid is integrated into the bacterial chromosome when it comes time to transfer, then it drags part or all of the bacterial genes along with it.

Once inside, the new bit of DNA finds the corresponding stretch of DNA in the resident chromosome and replaces it. This process is called homologous recombination, from the Greek for "agreeing in proportion." It is the same process by which the traits of parents, plant or animal, are mixed and redistributed to their children in sexually reproducing organisms: DNA molecules with nearly identical sequences exchange parts. It occurs in nearly all living cells. It is the basic purpose of sex.

Lederberg found several different strains of *E. coli* that could have sex this way (although some within the same species could not). He also found he could mate *E. coli* with several species in the genus *Shigella* and with one species of *Salmonella*, creating hybrid bacteria—and raising the question, once again, of how to define a species. Lederberg published his discovery of bacterial sex as his Ph.D. dissertation. In 1958 it brought him a Nobel Prize; years later this work was also hailed as the birth of biotechnology.

Zinder made an equally astonishing observation: he could transfer a genetic trait from one bacterium to another even when the two did not touch. The genetic engineer in this case is a kind of virus called a bacteriophage, or "eater of bacteria." Before recombinant DNA techniques were invented, bacteriophage—or simply phage—were a favorite for genetics experiments because they are so simple. They have as few as 4 genes, though more commonly they have 50 to 100. They are easy to grow in large numbers because they clone themselves inside the bacterial cell. One infecting phage makes hundreds or thousands of copies of itself inside a single bacterial cell—and a teaspoon of nutrient solution holds 100 million or more bacteria.

Zinder found that a phage could pick up hitchhiker genes from one bacterium and transport them to another. The bacterium he was studying was *Salmonella typhimurium*, a germ that gives mice the equivalent of typhoid fever. He and Lederberg had two mutant varieties of *S. typhimurium*, each unable to make certain amino acids and therefore crippled unless those nutrients were supplied to them. When they mixed a billion of each kind with bacteriophage, then spread them on a petri dish that contained no amino acids at all, a few colonies grew nevertheless. The bacteria acted as if their genes had been pooled. The same thing happened when one strain was resistant to the antibiotic streptomycin: the antibiotic resistance spread to the other strain. The phage, Zinder learned, packaged a piece of bacterial DNA into the virus particle instead of—or along with—its own DNA, and took it along when it infected the next cell. Zinder called this method of gene transfer "transduction."

A phage, like any virus, is not an organism in the usual sense. It is not a cell or collection of cells that extracts energy from chemicals to grow and move. A phage is a tiny packet of DNA wrapped in protein. Its protein coat protects it. It's also a DNA injector, whose purpose is to get the viral DNA from one cell to the next, where it can make a new crop of virus particles. Some bacteriophage look like lunar landing modules, their round heads full of DNA and connected by a stalk to spidery legs that attach to the bacterium. They are rather fantastic examples of self-organization: the whole process of viral assembly happens by itself. The proteins do what they are supposed to do by virtue of their structure. When enough of the DNA and of the structural proteins have been made inside the infected host cell, the head assembles itself and spools in a head-full of DNA.

Most of the time, only phage DNA is packaged. But every once in a while, a bit of bacterial DNA is pulled in and packed up. The machine just measures the length of DNA; it is blind to whether it is grabbing viral DNA or bacterial DNA. Released from the burst host cell, this transducing bacteriophage just as blindly does what all the other phage do: when it finds a new bacterial cell, it injects its DNA. But because its DNA is partly bacterial, it cannot make a full virus and so does not kill the cell. Instead the bacterial DNA finds its homolog in the new host and the bits of chromosomes recombine, just as in ordinary bacterial sex.

The ability of bacteriophage to assemble themselves from their protein subcomponents into a structure that can deliver and replicate its DNA became, in time, an essential part of the recombinant DNA toolkit . . .

Adding genes to plants required all the inventions and techniques just described. But to put a daffodil gene into rice also required the help of a natural genetic engineer, *Agrobacterium tumefasciens*. Only when this common soil bacterium was understood—and harnessed—did the genetic engineering of plants become a reality.

A. tumefasciens is closely related to *Rhizobium meliloti*, the bacterium that helps legumes like alfalfa and peas fix nitrogen. But rather than being helpful like its relative, *Agrobacterium* was known by 1907 to be an agricultural pest. It causes galls to form on fruit trees, walnuts, grapes, roses, and other valuable plants. Such tumors grow in places where the plant has been wounded. The cells in the gall produce chemicals that the bacteria use for food, so that *Agrobacterium* can be said to farm the plant without killing it. "For a long time, perhaps millions of years, the common soil bacterium *Agrobacterium tumefasciens* has been doing what molecular biologists are now striving to do," wrote Mary-Dell Chilton of the University of Washington in 1983. "It has been inserting foreign genes into plants and getting the plants to express those genes in the form of proteins."

That it was inserting *genes*—DNA—was not understood until the late 1970s. Thirty years before, Armin Braun of the Rockefeller Institute for Medical Research showed that *Agrobacterium* injected a tumor-inducing principle that transformed an ordinary plant cell into a constantly growing tumor cell. By analogy to the famous experiment done in 1928 by Fred Griffith, who showed that a deadly strain of the pneumonia bacterium could pass its virulence principle to a previously harmless one, French scientist Georges Morel predicted that this tumor-inducing principle of *Agrobacterium tumefasciens* would be DNA. But for a bacterium to transfer DNA to a plant— breaking the barrier not only between species, but between kingdoms—was almost unimaginable in the 1950s and 1960s.

In 1974 Jef Schell and Marc Van Montagu at the University of Ghent in Belgium discovered a large plasmid in the virulent strains of *Agrobacterium* that was missing in the harmless strains. The pest's method of operation began to become clear. A year later Mary-Dell Chilton, Milton Gordon, and Eugene Nester of the University of Washington confirmed that the plasmid was the tumor-inducing principle. *Agrobacterium* inserts a piece of the large plasmid into the plant's genome and tricks the plant into expressing it, manufacturing proteins that benefit the bacterium, but not the plant. The method it uses to transfer its genes, though, more closely resembles bacterial sex: *Agrobacterium* constructs a mating tube through which the plasmid travels.

When the complete genome of *Agrobacterium tumefaciens* was sequenced, it was found to have 5.67 million base pairs of DNA, an estimated 5,400 genes, on 4 structures: a circular chromosome, a linear chromosome, and 2 smaller circular plasmids. One of these plasmids is the genetic engineer. A short stretch of fewer than 80 genes, a region called *vir* for "virulence" is the critical part. It holds 7 groups of genes, or operons, labelled A through G, each containing from 1 to 11 genes. The first operon, *virA*, encodes a protein that sits on the bacterium's cell membrane. It senses the chemicals released when a plant cell is injured, and immediately signals *virG*, whose job it is to turn on the other genes in the *vir* region. The *virB* proteins create the connecting tube. A protein encoded by *virD* nicks the plasmid's DNA strand in two particular spots, releasing a long bit of single-stranded DNA known as the Transfer-DNA, or T-DNA. The *virE* proteins then coat the T-DNA and usher it through the mating tube and into the plant cell and thence to its nucleus. There the T-DNA seeks out and links up with the plant cell's nuclear DNA, permanently transforming the plant cell into a tumor cell.

On the single-stranded stretch that is transferred, Chilton and her colleagues found a transposon. It was "a sizable piece of DNA," she wrote. "Its presence in the tumor cells meant that a large segment of foreign DNA, enough to carry several genes, can be transferred along with the T-DNA."

Four laboratories began working immediately on the idea of using *Agrobacterium* as a vector: Schell and Van Montagu at the University of Ghent in Belgium, Eugene Nester at the University of Washington in Seattle, Mary-Dell Chilton at Washington University in St. Louis, and Rob Horsch and his colleagues at Monsanto. They announced their success simultaneously in 1983. The goal of these experiments had been to see if the *Agrobacterium* plasmid could be used to introduce a gene—any gene—into a plant. To show that it could be done, a gene that makes bacteria resistant to the antibiotic kanamycin was substituted for the tumor-forming genes. Kanamycin kills plant cells—it interferes with their ability to make proteins. Without the new gene, all of the plant cells in the experiment would die if they were exposed to the antibiotic. The techniques used to construct the recombinant *Agrobacterium* plasmid were similar to those that Cohen and Boyer used (although a bit more complicated because the *Agrobacterium* plasmid was so very large).

Bits of tobacco leaves were then dipped into a suspension of *Agrobacterium* containing the recombinant plasmid carrying the kanamycin-resistance gene. The infected leaf bits were put on agar that contained growth hormones, which allowed the cells to grow into a disorganized callus. The agar medium also contained kanamycin, which prevented the growth of cells that lacked the recombinant plasmid. Gradually the callus cultures were weaned off growth hormones and began to produce shoots, then roots. The plants not only grew on the antibiotic, the DNA that codes for kanamycin resistance was now linked to tobacco DNA—and plant genetic engineering was born.

. . . Regardless of the technique that gets the DNA into the plant, the result is a DNA chimera: a piece of foreign DNA is spliced into the plant's genome. As Boyer and Cohen noted when they coined the term in 1973, a DNA chimera is no different than the chimeras that have been created for the last 3,000 or so years by grafting. It is as natural—or as artificial— as an apple tree. Neither would exist, in their current forms, without human intervention. They differ only in scale: the genetically engineered plant is created using molecular scissors—restriction enzymes—not a knife or scalpel. What's grafted on is a few well-studied genes, not a bud or a branch. Each technique combines genes from different species. Even crossing kingdoms to put a bacterial gene into a plant is not new: *Agrobacterium* has done it for millennia. What's new is that the pool of possible genes from which plant breeders can now choose has grown very much larger.

James D. Watson, along with his research partner, Francis Crick, is credited with first discovering the double-helix structure of DNA. The article in which the two scientists announced their landmark discovery was published in the April 2, 1953, issue of the respected British science journal Nature. *In 1962, Watson shared the Nobel Prize in Physiology or Medicine with Crick and a third scientist, Maurice Wilkins.*

For many years, Watson has been a strong proponent of biotechnology, and has been especially active in promoting GM crops, believing that the benefits of the technology outweigh any risks. In his book DNA: The Secret of Life, *Watson stays true to his role in promoting genetic engineering and its applications in today's world. In the following excerpt from "Tempest in a Cereal Box," the book's chapter on GM crops, Watson presents the advantages of these new plants. —SG*

From *DNA: The Secret of Life*
by James D. Watson
2003

At first *Agrobacterium* was thought to work its devious magic only on certain plants. Among these, we could not, alas, count the agriculturally important group that includes cereals such as corn, wheat, and rice. However, in the years since it gave birth to plant genetic engineering, *Agrobacterium* has itself been the focus of genetic engineers, and technical advances have extended its empire to even the most recalcitrant crop species. Before these innovations, we had to rely upon a rather more haphazard, but no less effective, way of getting our DNA selection into a corn, wheat, or rice cell. The desired gene is affixed to tiny gold or tungsten pellets, which are literally fired like bullets into the cell. The trick is to fire the pellets with enough force to enter the cell, but not so much that they will exit the other side! The method lacks *Agrobacterium*'s finesse, but it does get the job done.

This "gene gun" was developed during the early 1980s by John Sanford at Cornell's Agricultural Research Station. Sanford chose to experiment with onions because of their conveniently large cells; he recalls that the combination of blasted onions and gunpowder made his lab smell like a McDonald's franchise on a firing range. Initial reactions to his concept were incredulous, but in 1987 Sanford unveiled his botanical firearm in the pages of *Nature*. By 1990, scientists had succeeded in using the gun to shoot new genes into corn, America's most important food crop, worth $19 billion in 2001 alone.

Corn is not only a valuable food crop; unique among major American crops, it also has long been a valuable seed crop. The seed business has traditionally been something of a financial dead-end: a farmer buys your seed, but then for sub-sequent plantings he can take seed from the crop he has just grown, so he never needs to buy your seed again. American corn seed companies solved the problem of nonrepeat business in the twenties by marketing hybrid corn, each hybrid the product of a cross between two particular genetic lines of corn. The hybrid's characteristic high yield makes it attractive to farmers. Because of the Mendelian mechanics of breeding, the strategy of using seed from the crop itself (i.e., the product of a hybrid × hybrid cross) fails because most of the seed will lack those high-yield characteristics of the original hybrid. Farmers therefore must return to the seed company every year for a new batch of high-yield hybrid seed.

America's biggest hybrid corn seed company, Pioneer Hi-Bred International (now owned by Du Pont), has long been a midwestern institution. Today it controls about 40 percent of the U.S. corn seed market, with $1 billion in annual sales. Founded in 1926 by Henry Wallace, who went on to become Franklin D. Roosevelt's vice president, the company used to hire as many as forty thousand high-schoolers every summer to ensure the hybridity of its hybrid corn. The two parental strains were grown in neighboring stands, and then these "detasselers" removed by hand the male pollen-producing flowers (tassels) before they became mature from one of the two strains. Therefore, only the other strain could serve as a possible source of pollen, so all the seed produced by the detasseled strain was sure to be hybrid. Even today, detasseling provides summer work for thousands: in July 2002, Pioneer hired thirty-five thousand temps for the job.

One of Pioneer's earliest customers was, Roswell Garst, an Iowa farmer who, impressed by Wallace's hybrids, bought a license to sell Pioneer seed corn. On September 23, 1959, in one of the less frigid moments of the Cold War the Soviet leader Nikita Khrushchev visited Garst's farm to learn more about the American agricultural miracle and the hybrid corn behind it. The nation Khrushchev had inherited from Stalin had neglected agriculture in the drive toward industrialization, and the new premier was keen to make amends. In 1961, the incoming Kennedy administration approved the sale to the Soviets of corn seed, agricultural equipment, and fertilizer, all of which contributed to the doubling of Soviet corn production in just two years . . .

Weeds are difficult to eliminate. Like the crop whose growth they inhibit, they are plants too. How do you kill weeds without killing your crop? Ideally, there would be some kind of pass-over system whereby every plant lacking a "protective mark"—the weeds, in this case—would be killed, while those possessing the mark—the crop—would be spared. Genetic engineering has furnished farmers and gardeners just such a system in the form of Monsanto's "Roundup Ready" technology. "Roundup" is a broad-spectrum herbicide that can kill almost any plant. But through genetic alteration Monsanto scientists have also produced "Roundup Ready" crops that possess built-in resistance to the herbicide, and do just fine as all the weeds around them are biting the dust. Of course, it suits the company's commercial interests that farmers who buy Monsanto's adapted seed will buy Monsanto's herbicide as well. But such an approach is also actually beneficial to the environment. Normally a farmer must use a range of different weed killers, each one toxic to a particular group of weeds but safe for the crop. There are many potential weed groups to guard against. Using a single herbicide for all the weeds in creation actually reduces the environmental levels of such chemicals, and Roundup itself is rapidly degraded in the soil.

Unfortunately, the rise of agriculture was a boon not only to our ancestors but to herbivorous insects as well. Imagine being an insect that eats wheat and related wild grasses. Once upon a time, thousands of years ago, you had to forage far and wide for your dinner. Then along came agriculture, and humans conveniently started laying out dinner in enormous stands. It is not surprising that crops have to be defended against insect attack. From the elimination point of view at least, insects pose less of a problem than weeds because it is possible to devise poisons that target animals, not plants. The trouble is that humans and other creatures we value are animals as well.

The full extent of the risks involved with the use of pesticides was not widely apparent until Rachel Carson first documented them. The impact on the environment of long-lived chlorine-containing pesticides like DDT (banned in Europe and North America since 1972) has been devastating. In addition, there is a danger that residues from these pesticides will wind up in our food. While these chemicals at low dosage may not be lethal—they were, after all, designed to kill animals at a considerable evolutionary remove from us—there remain concerns about possible mutagenic effects, resulting in human cancers and birth defects. An alternative to DDT came in the form of a group of organophosphate pesticides, like parathion. In their favor, they decompose rapidly once applied and do not linger in the environment. On the other hand, they are even more acutely toxic than DDT; the sarin nerve gas used in the terrorist attack on the Tokyo subway system in 1995, for instance, is a member of the organophosphate group.

Even solutions using nature's own chemicals have produced a backlash. In the mid-1960s, chemical companies began developing synthetic versions of a natural insecticide, pyrethrin, derived from a small daisylike chrysanthemum. These helped keep farm pests in check for more than a decade until, not surprisingly, their widespread use led to the emergence of resistant insect populations. Even more troubling, however, pyrethrin, though natural, is not necessarily good for humans; in fact, like many plant-derived substances it can be quite toxic. Pyrethrin experiments with rats have produced Parkinson-like symptoms, and epidemiologists have noted that this disease has a higher incidence in rural environments than in urban ones. Overall—and there is a dearth of reliable data—the Environmental Protection Agency estimates that there may be as many as 300,000 pesticide-related illnesses among U.S. farmworkers every year.

Organic farmers have always had their tricks for avoiding pesticides. One ingenious organic method relies on a toxin derived from a bacterium—or, often, the bacterium itself—to protect plants from insect attack. *Bacillus thuringiensis* (Bt) naturally assaults the cells of insect intestines, feasting upon the nutrients released by the damaged cells. The guts of the insects exposed to the bacterium are paralyzed causing the creatures to die from the combined effects of starvation and tissue damage. Originally identified in 1901, when it decimated Japan's silkworm population, *Bacillus thuringiensis* was not so named until 1911, during an outbreak among flour moths in the German province of Thuringia. First used as a pesticide in France in 1938, the bacterium was originally thought to work only against lepidopteran (moth/butterfly) caterpillars, but different strains have subsequently proved effective against the larvae of beetles and flies. Best of all, the bacterium is insect-specific: most animal intestines are acidic—that is, low pH—but the insect larval gut is highly alkaline—high pH—just the environment in which the pernicious Bt toxin is activated.

In the age of recombinant DNA technology the success of
Bacillus thuringiensis as a pesticide has inspired genetic engineers. What if, instead of applying the bacterium scattershot
to crops, the gene for the Bt toxin were engineered into the
genome of crop plants? The farmer would never again need to
dust his crops because every mouthful of the plant would be
lethal to the insect ingesting it (and harmless to us). The
method has at least two clear advantages over the traditional
dumping of pesticides on crops. First, only insects that actually eat the crop will be exposed to the pesticide; non-pests
are not harmed, as they would be with external application.
Second, implanting the Bt toxin gene into the plant genome
causes it to be produced by every cell of the plant; traditional
pesticides are typically applied only to the leaf and stem. And
so bugs that feed on the roots or that bore inside plant tissues,
formerly immune to externally applied pesticides, are now also
condemned to a Bt death.

Today we have a whole range of Bt designer crops,
including "Bt corn," "Bt potato," "Bt cotton," and "Bt soybean," and the net effect has been a massive reduction in the
use of pesticides. In 1995 cotton farmers in the Mississippi
Delta sprayed their fields an average of 4.5 times per season.
Just one year later, as Bt cotton caught on, that average—for
all farms, including those planting non-Bt cotton varieties—
dropped to 2.5 times. It is estimated that since 1996 the use
of Bt crops has resulted in an annual reduction of 2 million
gallons of pesticides in the United States. I have not visited
cotton country lately but I would wager that billboards there
are no longer hawking chemical insect-killers; in fact, I sus-
pect that Burma-Shave ads are more likely to make a

comeback than ones for pesticides. And other countries are starting to benefit as well: in China in 1999 the planting of Bt cotton reduced pesticide use by an estimated 1,300 *tons*.

Biotechnology has also fortified plants against other traditional enemies in a surprising form of disease prevention superficially similar to vaccination. We inject our children with mild forms of various pathogens to induce an immune response that will protect them against infection when they are exposed to the disease. Remarkably when a plant, which has no immune system properly speaking, has been exposed to a particular virus, it often becomes resistant to other strains of the same virus. Roger Beachy at Washington University in St. Louis, realized that this phenomenon of "cross-protection" might allow genetic engineers to "immunize" plants against threatening diseases. He tried inserting the gene for the virus's protein coat into the plants to see whether this might induce cross-protection without exposure to the virus itself. It did indeed. Somehow the presence in the cell of the viral coat protein prevents the cell from being taken over by invading viruses.

Beachy's method saved the Hawaiian papaya business. Between 1993 and 1997, production declined by 40 percent thanks to an invasion of the papaya ringspot virus; one of the islands' major industries was thus threatened with extinction. By inserting a gene for just part of the virus's coat protein into the papayas genome, scientists were able to create plants resistant to attacks by the virus. Hawaii's papayas lived to fight another day.

Scientists at Monsanto later applied the same harmless method to combat a common disease caused by potato virus X.

(Potato viruses are unimaginatively named. There is also a potato virus Y.) Unfortunately, McDonald's and other major players in the burger business feared the use of such modified spuds would lead to boycotts organized by the anti-GM food partisans. Consequently the fries they now serve cost more than they should . . .

In addition to defending a plant against its enemies, biotechnology can also help bring a more desirable product to market. Unfortunately however, sometimes the cleverest biotechnologists can fail to see the forest for the trees (or the crop for the fruits). So it was with Calgene, an innovative California-based company. In 1994 Calgene earned the distinction of producing the very first GM product to reach supermarket shelves. Calgene had solved a major problem of tomato growing: how to bring ripe fruit to market instead of picking them when green, as is customary. But in their technical triumph they forgot fundamentals: their rather unfortunately named "Flavr-Savr" tomato was neither tasty nor cheap enough to succeed. And so it was that the tomato had the added distinction of being one of the first GM products to disappear from supermarket shelves.

Still, the technology was ingenious. Tomato ripening is naturally accompanied by softening, thanks to the gene encoding an enzyme called polygalacturonase (PG), which softens the fruit by breaking down the cell walls. Because soft tomatoes do not travel well, the fruit are typically picked when they are still green (and firm) and then reddened using ethene gas, a ripening agent. Calgene researchers figured that knocking out the PG gene would result in fruit that stayed firm longer, even after ripening on the vine. They inserted an inverted copy of the PG gene, which, owing to the affinities between complementary base pairs, had the effect of causing the RNA produced by the PG gene proper to become "bound up" with the RNA produced by the inverted gene, thus neutralizing the former's capacity to create the softening enzyme. The lack of PG function meant that the tomato stayed firmer, and so it was now possible in principle to deliver fresher, riper tomatoes to supermarket shelves. But Calgene, triumphant in its molecular wizardry, underestimated the trickiness of basic tomato farming. (As one grower hired by the company commented, "Put a molecular biologist out on a farm, and he'd starve to death.") The strain of tomato Calgene had chosen to enhance was a particularly bland and tasteless one: there simply was not much "flavr" to save, let alone savor. The tomato was a technological triumph but a commercial failure.

Overall, plant technology's most potentially important contribution to human well-being may involve enhancing the nutrient profile of crop plants, compensating for their natural shortcomings as sources of nourishment. Because plants are typically low in amino acids essential for human life, those who eat a purely vegetarian diet, among whom we may count most of the developing world, may suffer from amino acid deficiencies. Genetic engineering can ensure that crops contain a fuller array of nutrients, including amino acids, than the unmodified versions that would otherwise be grown and eaten in these parts of the world.

To take an example, in 1992 UNICEF estimated that some 124 million children around the world were dangerously deficient in vitamin A. The annual result is some half million cases of childhood blindness; many of these children will even die for want of the vitamin. Since rice does not contain vitamin A or its biochemical precursors, these deficient populations are concentrated in parts of the world where rice is the staple diet.

An international effort, funded largely by the Rockefeller Foundation (a nonprofit organization and therefore protected from the charges of commercialism or exploitation often leveled at producers of GM foods), has developed what has come to be called "golden rice." Though this rice doesn't contain vitamin A per se, it yields a critical precursor, beta-carotene (which gives carrots their bright orange color and golden rice the fainter orange tint that inspired its name). As those involved in humanitarian relief have learned, however, malnutrition can be more complex than a single deficiency: the absorption of vitamin A precursors in the gut works best in the presence of fat, but the malnourished whom the golden rice was designed to help often have little or no fat in their diet. Nevertheless golden rice represents at least one step in the right direction. It is here that we see the broader promise of GM agriculture to diminish human suffering.

We are merely at the beginning of a great GM plant revolution, only starting to see the astonishing range of potential applications. Apart from delivering nutrients where they are wanting, plants may also one day hold the key to distributing orally administered vaccine proteins. By simply engineering a banana that produces, say the polio vaccine protein—which would remain intact in the fruit, which travels well and is most often eaten uncooked—we could one day distribute the vaccine to parts of the world that lack public health infrastructure. Plants may also serve less vital but still immensely helpful purposes. One company for example, has succeeded in inducing cotton plants to produce a form of polyester, thereby creating a natural cotton-polyester blend. With such potential to reduce our dependence on chemical manufacturing processes (of which polyester fabrication is but one) and their polluting by-products, plant engineering will provide ways as yet unimagined to preserve the environment.

———■———

Norman Borlaug is often referred to as the father of the green revolution. He was awarded the 1970 Nobel Peace Prize for a lifetime of work devoted to ending world hunger; and he is credited with saving millions of lives through his agricultural projects all over the world. He sees food supply as critical to building effective health and educational systems, strong economies, and national stability. He has stressed these points repeatedly in the hundreds of speeches and interviews he has given through his more than six-decades-long career.

In the following excerpt from an interview with Ronald Bailey of Reason *magazine, Borlaug addresses the European resistance to genetically modified crops and the claims of activists and environmentalists who disagree with the genetic engineering of food sources. He believes such opposition is rooted in fear of change. In Borlaug's opinion, genetically modified crops, more resilient and nutritious than their non-GM counterparts, allow countries with millions of hungry citizens to become self-sufficient in providing for their citizens. —SG*

From "Billions Served"
by Ronald Bailey
Reason, April 2000

Who has saved more human lives than anyone else in history? Who won the Nobel Peace Prize in 1970? Who still teaches at Texas A&M at the age of 86? The answer is Norman Borlaug.

Who? Norman Borlaug, the father of the "Green Revolution," the dramatic improvement in agricultural productivity that swept the globe in the 1960s.

Borlaug grew up on a small farm in Iowa and graduated from the University of Minnesota, where he studied forestry and plant pathology, in the 1930s. In 1944, the Rockefeller Foundation invited him to work on a project to boost wheat production in Mexico. At the time Mexico was importing a good share of its grain. Borlaug and his staff in Mexico spent nearly 20 years breeding the high-yield dwarf wheat that sparked the Green Revolution, the transformation that forestalled the mass starvation predicted by neo-Malthusians.

In the late 1960s, most experts were speaking of imminent global famines in which billions would perish. "The battle to feed all of humanity is over," biologist Paul Ehrlich famously wrote in his 1968 bestseller *The Population Bomb*. "In the 1970s and 1980s hundreds of millions of people will starve to death in spite of any crash programs embarked upon now." Ehrlich also said, "I have yet to meet anyone familiar with the situation who thinks India will be self-sufficient in food by 1971." He insisted that "India couldn't possibly feed two hundred million more people by 1980."

But Borlaug and his team were already engaged in the kind of crash program that Ehrlich declared wouldn't work. Their dwarf wheat varieties resisted a wide spectrum of plant pests and diseases and produced two to three times more grain than the traditional varieties. In 1965, they had begun a massive campaign to ship the miracle wheat to Pakistan and India and teach local farmers how to cultivate it properly. By 1968, when Ehrlich's book appeared, the U.S. Agency for International Development had already hailed Borlaug's achievement as a "Green Revolution."

In Pakistan, wheat yields rose from 4.6 million tons in 1965 to 8.4 million in 1970. In India, they rose from 12.3 million tons to 20 million. And the yields continue to increase. Last year, India harvested a record 73.5 million tons of wheat, up 11.5 percent from 1998. Since Ehrlich's dire predictions in 1968, India's population has more than doubled, its wheat production has more than tripled, and its economy has grown nine-fold. Soon after Borlaug's success with wheat, his colleagues at the Consultative Group on International Agricultural Research developed high-yield rice varieties that quickly spread the Green Revolution through most of Asia . . .

REASON Science Correspondent Ronald Bailey met with Borlaug at Texas A&M, where he is Distinguished Professor in the Soil and Crop Sciences Department . . .

Reason: Could genetically engineered crops help farmers in developing countries?

Borlaug: Biotech has a big potential in Africa, not immediately, but down the road. Five to eight years from now, parts of it will play a role there. Take the case of maize with the gene that controls the tolerance level for the weed killer

Roundup. Roundup kills all the weeds, but it's short-lived, so it doesn't have any residual effect, and from that standpoint it's safe for people and the environment. The gene for herbicide tolerance is built into the crop variety, so that when a farmer sprays he kills only weeds but not the crops. Roundup Ready soybeans and corn are being very widely used in the U.S. and Argentina. At this stage, we haven't used varieties with the tolerance for Roundup or any other weed killer [in Africa], but it will have a role to play.

Roundup Ready crops could be used in zero-tillage cultivation in African countries. In zero tillage, you leave the straw, the rice, the wheat if it's at high elevation, or most of the corn stock, remove only what's needed for animal feed, and plant directly [without plowing], because this will cut down erosion. Central African farmers don't have any animal power, because sleeping sickness kills all the animals—cattle, the horses, the burros and the mules. So draft animals don't exist, and farming is all by hand and the hand tools are hoes and machetes. Such hand tools are not very effective against the aggressive tropical grasses that typically invade farm fields. Some of those grasses have sharp spines on them, and they're not very edible. They invade the cornfields, and it gets so bad that farmers must abandon the fields for a while, move on, and clear some more forest. That's the way it's been going on for centuries, slash-and-burn farming. But with this kind of weed killer, Roundup, you can clear the fields of these invasive grasses and plant directly if you have the herbicide-tolerance gene in the crop plants.

Reason: Does the European ban on biotechnology encourage elites in developing countries to say, "Well, if it's not good enough for Europeans, it's not good enough for my people"?

Borlaug: Of course. This is a negative effect. We always have this. Take the case of DDT. When it was banned here in the U.S. and the European countries, I testified about the value of DDT for malaria control, especially throughout Africa and in many parts of Asia. The point I made in my testimony as a witness for the USDA was that if you ban DDT here in the U.S., where you don't have these problems, then OK, you've got other insecticides for agriculture, but when you ban it here and then exert pressures on heads of government in Africa and Asia, that's another matter. They've got serious human and animal diseases, and DDT is important. Of course, they did ban DDT, and the danger is that they will do the same thing with biotech now.

Reason: What do you see as the future of biotechnology in agriculture?

Borlaug: Biotechnology will help us do things that we couldn't do before, and do it in a more precise and safe way. Biotechnology will allow us to cross genetic barriers that we were never able to cross with conventional genetics and plant breeding. In the past, conventional plant breeders were forced to bring along many other genes with the genes, say, for insect or disease resistance that we wanted to incorporate in a new crop variety. These extra genes often had negative effects, and it took years of breeding to remove them. Conventional plant breeding is crude in comparison to the methods that are being used with genetic engineering. However, I believe that we have done a poor job of explaining the complexities and the importance of biotechnology to the general public.

Reason: A lot of activists say that it's wrong to cross genetic barriers between species. Do you agree?

Borlaug: No. As a matter of fact, Mother Nature has crossed species barriers, and sometimes nature crosses barriers between genera—that is, between unrelated groups of species. Take the case of wheat. It is the result of a natural cross made by Mother Nature long before there was scientific man. Today's modern red wheat variety is made up of three groups of seven chromosomes, and each of those three groups of seven chromosomes came from a different wild grass. First, Mother Nature crossed two of the grasses, and this cross became the durum wheats, which were the commercial grains of the first civilizations spanning from Sumeria until well into the Roman period. Then Mother Nature crossed that 14-chromosome durum wheat with another wild wheat grass to create what was essentially modern wheat at the time of the Roman Empire.

Durum wheat was OK for making flat Arab bread, but it didn't have elastic gluten. The thing that makes modern wheat different from all of the other cereals is that it has two proteins that give it the doughy quality when it's mixed with water. Durum wheats don't have gluten, and that's why we use them to make spaghetti today. The second cross of durum wheat with the other wild wheat produced a wheat whose dough could be fermented with yeast to produce a big loaf. So modern bread wheat is the result of crossing three species barriers, a kind of natural genetic engineering.

Reason: Environmentalists say agricultural biotech will harm biodiversity.

Borlaug: I don't believe that. If we grow our food and fiber on the land best suited to farming with the technology that we have and what's coming, including proper use of genetic engineering and biotechnology, we will leave untouched vast tracts of land, with all of their plant and animal diversity. It is because we use farmland so effectively now that President Clinton was recently able to set aside another 50 or 60 million acres of land as wilderness areas. That would not have been possible had it not been for the efficiency of modern agriculture.

In 1960, the production of the 17 most important food, feed, and fiber crops—virtually all of the important crops grown in the U.S. at that time and still grown today—was 252 million tons. By 1990, it had more than doubled, to 596 million tons, and was produced on 25 million fewer acres than were cultivated in 1960. If we had tried to produce the harvest of 1990 with the technology of 1960, we would have had to have increased the cultivated area by another 177 million hectares, about 460 million more acres of land of the same quality—which we didn't have, and so it would have been much more. We would have moved into marginal grazing areas and plowed up things that wouldn't be productive in the long run. We would have had to move into rolling mountainous country and chop down our forests. President Clinton would not have had the nice job of setting aside millions of acres of land for restricted use, where you can't cut a tree even for paper and pulp or for lumber. So all of this ties together . . .

Reason: Some activists claim that herbicide-resistant crops end up increasing the amount of herbicide that's sprayed on fields. Do you think that's true?

Borlaug: Look, insecticides, herbicides, and fertilizer cost money, and the farmer doesn't have much margin. He's going to try to use the minimum amount that he can get by with. Probably in most cases, a farmer applies less than he should. I don't think farmers are likely to use too much.

Reason: What other crop pests might biotech control in the future?

Borlaug: All of the cereals except rice are susceptible to one to three different species of rust fungi. Now, rusts are obligate parasites. They can only live under green tissue, but they are long-lived. They can move in the air sometimes 100, 500, 800 miles, and they get in the jet stream and fall. If the crop variety is susceptible to rust fungi and moisture is there and the temperature is right, it's like lighting a fire. It just destroys crops. But rice isn't susceptible—no rust . . . One thing that I hope to live to see is somebody taking that block of rust-resistance genes in rice and putting it into all of the other cereals.

Reason: Do biotech crops pose a health risk to human beings?

Borlaug: I see no difference between the varieties carrying a BT gene or a herbicide resistance gene, or other genes that will come to be incorporated, and the varieties created by conventional plant breeding. I think the activists have blown the health risks of biotech all out of proportion.

Reason: You mentioned that you are afraid that the doomsayers could stop the progress in food production.

Borlaug: It worries me, if they gum up all of these developments. It's elitism, and the American people are vulnerable to this, too. I'm talking about the extremists here and in Western Europe . . . In the U.S., 98 percent of consumers live in cities or urban areas or good-size towns. Only 2 percent still live out there on the land. In Western Europe also, a big percentage of the people live off the farms, and they don't understand the complexities of agriculture. So they are easily swayed by these scare stories that we are on the verge of being poisoned out of existence by farm chemicals.

Bruce Ames, the head of biochemistry at Berkeley, has analyzed hundreds and hundreds of foods, including all of the basic ones that we have been eating from the beginning of agriculture up to the present time. He has found that they contain trace amounts of many completely natural chemical compounds that are toxic or carcinogenic, but they're present in such small quantities that they apparently don't affect us.

Reason: Would you say the Green Revolution was a success?

Borlaug: Yes, but it's a never-ending job. When I was born in 1914, the world population was approximately 1.6 billion people. It has just turned 6 billion. We've had no major famines any place in the world since the Green Revolution began. We've had local famines where these African wars have been going on and are still going on. However, if we could get the infrastructure straightened out in African countries south of the Sahara, you could end hunger there pretty fast . . . And if you look at the data that's put out by the World Health Organization and [the U.N.'s Food and Agriculture Organization], there are probably 800 million people who are undernourished in the world. So there's still a lot of work to do.

CHAPTER TWO

SCIENCE, TECHNOLOGY, AND SOCIETY: FOOD FOR EARTH

Perhaps the most important survival adaptation that plants have is diversity within species. This ensures survival of the species should something threaten one strain. If disease or changes to the environment should make it impossible for one strain of the plant to grow, then another strain will replace the weaker variant and the species will survive.

An example of what can happen when a species becomes reduced to just one strain is illustrated by the failure of potato crops in Ireland during the mid-nineteenth century. During that time, the potato was a staple crop, and its heartiness assured the Irish of food in even the bleakest of times. Then, suddenly, a foreign and unforeseeable devastation arrived from mainland Europe. The bacteria Phytophthora infestans *wiped out the single strain of potato in Ireland in one fell swoop.*

Today, many worry about the effect of GM technology on plant diversity. In the following excerpt, acclaimed journalist Peter Pringle examines the importance of biodiversity to plant survival—and the survival of the human beings who depend upon those plants. **—SG**

From *Food, Inc.: Mendel to Monsanto— The Promises and Perils of the Biotech Harvest*
by Peter Pringle
2003

To boost yields of wheat and rice, Japanese farmers pioneered the industrial agriculture so reviled by environmentalists and ecologists today. They started using commercial fertilizer— mainly organic soybean cake—which suited their new varieties but required deep plowing. This meant new plow designs and the use of draft animals instead of human labor. It also meant new irrigation systems, because the fields had to be drained before they could be plowed. Japanese farmers also introduced double-cropping—planting two separate crops a year on the same field. The more they doused the wheat and rice plants with fertilizers, the heavier the ears and panicles became, until they fell over. The farmers discovered that this lodging could be prevented if the plant were a dwarf with a shorter and sturdier stem.

As early as the beginning of the Meiji Restoration— around 1868—Japanese agriculture had changed dramatically with the introduction of dwarf varieties. By the end of the nineteenth century the Japanese were breeding the most efficient food crops in the world; it would be several decades before the West matched their scientific advances. Some of the more famous dwarfs would come from Taiwan, having survived Japanese efforts to extinguish them. An early rice favorite was called *shinriki*, which in Japanese means "power of the gods."

At first, Westerners had viewed the Japanese obsession with dwarf plants as a mere curiosity, like their miniature gardens. When Horace Capron, the U.S. Commissioner of Agriculture, visited Japan in 1873, he wrote home, "The Japanese farmers have brought the art of dwarfing to perfection." But he didn't bother to send any seeds to farmers back home. At the time, American farmers judged plants mostly by size. They were proud of their hefty varieties, showing them off at annual shows. In the Corn Belt the criteria for a fine ear of corn were to a large extent how it looked—its size, shape, color, silky tips, and all. Like the old hunter gatherers, Americans preferred a tasty-looking crop. Big produce won the prizes in the county fairs. An ideal ear of corn was ten and a half inches in length and seven and a half inches in circumference, with nice, plump kernels that had "well-rounded butts."

At the turn of the century, the Division of Botany of the U.S. Department of Agriculture decided that dwarf plants in Japan deserved a closer look. Professor Seaman Knapp of Iowa State University was dispatched to Japan. He sent home two tons of rice seed, including the famous short-grained and god-powered *shinriki*. The new varieties were planted in the Carolinas and Louisiana. *Shinriki* produced high yields but was eventually abandoned in favor of a longer-grained Honduran rice. The American obsession with size applied even to the length of the grain.

Japanese dwarf varieties would not make a decisive contribution to American agriculture until after World War II. General Douglas MacArthur's occupation force in Japan included U.S. government officials advising the Japanese on how to put their war-ravaged economy back together again.

One of these officials was a U.S. Department of Agriculture employee named Cecil Salmon, who spotted the same dwarf wheat and rice seen seventy years earlier by Commissioner Capron. One in particular, a variety of wheat named *Norin 10*, caught Salmon's eye. He sent back some seeds for experimental sowing.

Norin 10, as it turned out, was part American. Japanese plant breeders had created this variety in 1917 as a cross between a local dwarf and an American wheat variety named *Fultz* after its breeder, Abraham Fultz, a Pennsylvania wheat farmer. The *Fultz* wheat was itself the product of generations of careful selection by American farmers, but only the Japanese had realized its full potential. After World War II, the dwarfing genes of *Norin 10* and other Japanese types were quickly incorporated into U.S. varieties and then into the Green Revolution. In the postwar developing world millions of lives were at risk from starvation, and in a stunning triumph for technology, the United States would deliver the latest farming techniques and improved varieties of staple crops free of charge to undeveloped nations in Latin America and Asia.

To critics of the Green Revolution, the dwarf varieties would become a symbol of the basic flaw in the new system of modern agriculture—the creation of monocultures, or single variety, genetically uniform crops vulnerable to disease. *Taipei 309* would become a target of the antibiotech forces because it was a product of the Green Revolution and part of what one critic called "the plague of sameness." That plague brought one variety of food plant to millions of acres worldwide, one type of agriculture for the developed world and the same type for the undeveloped world. Before long, it seemed, there would be only one lonely variety of cabbage and one solitary type of cucumber.

Monocultures inevitably squeezed out the local traditional varieties that had fed, housed, clothed, and cured people throughout history. Scientists invented new terms to fit the passing of so many ancient plants—*genetic erosion* and *loss of biodiversity*. Over time, these terms would become political slogans as well as descriptions of ecological phenomena.

The ancient gene pools of the lost plants held raw materials essential for making the farming revolution. To plant breeders, access to these endangered gene pools was like access to oil wells for motor cars. If there was no gene pool to provide a constant flow of new and different genes to keep a cultivated plant healthy and robust, the plant's useful life, at least to humans, was over.

The alarm about sameness had been raised early in the United States. The 1936 U.S. Department of Agriculture Yearbook warned, "In the hinterlands of Asia there were probably barley fields when man was young. The progenies of these fields with all their surviving variations constitute the world's priceless reservoir of germ plasm. It has waited through long centuries. Unfortunately, from the breeder's standpoint, it is now imperiled . . . When new barleys replace those grown by the farmers of Ethiopia or Tibet, the world will have lost something irreplaceable."

The real fear, however, was the loss of these gene pools in the early centers of human civilization where the staples had been cultivated—the Middle East, India, Southeast Asia, Mexico, and Peru, the so-called centers of diversity of food plants. In those dozen or so centers, the cultivation of plants by early farmers had produced thousands of different varieties, but none of the key centers was in the developed world. Plant breeders were constantly launching expeditions to tropical countries to discover one more exotic gene.

In exchange for giving away their technology American seed companies would gain access through the Green Revolution to these invaluable gene pools. The U.S. program's humanitarian goal was the conquest of hunger, but as University of Wisconsin rural sociologist Jack Kloppenberg commented, the overall strategy for spreading the Green Revolution was a "volatile mix of business, philanthropy, science, and politics."

A green revolution today suggests a radical environmental movement, but this one was nothing of the kind. Toward the end of World War II, the United States decided to use its dominance in world food production to extend its global influence. Food would become a political device. In a dual strategy the United States would simultaneously fight world hunger and halt the spread of communism. Population explosions in the undeveloped nations of Latin America and Asia meant there was not enough to eat. Hunger led to social upheaval that could leave nations vulnerable to communist takeover. The Roosevelt administration was especially concerned about political stability on America's southern border. Mexican agriculture was in crisis, and the United States feared a peasant uprising.

At the time there was no United Nations or coordinated international aid program to help countries improve the yield of their crops. The U.S. administration launched its Good Neighbor policy promoting U.S. interests without military intervention. Two of America's leading philanthropic foundations, Rockefeller and Ford, put together an emergency crop improvement program, first in Mexico and then in the rest of Latin America, in India in the 1960s, and in other developing nations in Asia in the 1970s.

When it was over, an enterprising U.S. government bureaucrat from the Agency for International Development would describe this boom in staple crops as the "Green Revolution." *Green* referred to swaths of young green shoots of corn, wheat, and rice that suddenly took hold in lands that had previously produced sparse harvests. *Revolution* referred not to upheaval of the masses but to the combined effect of improved seeds, chemical fertilizers and pesticides, and water irrigation projects. The true birthplace of the revolution, however, was not Mexico or Colombia, the Philippines or Surinam, but the experimental farms of the advanced industrialized nations, first Japan, then the United States and Europe.

. . . Producing enough food to stay ahead of the increase in world population was the daunting mission of a small number of dedicated plant breeders around the world. The most famous American was Norman Borlaug, a Midwesterner and plant pathologist who oversaw the Rockefeller Foundation's wheat program in those early years of the Green Revolution. Borlaug's first task was to breed wheat varieties that were resistant to disease, especially the debilitating wheat stem rust. Mexico's wheats had lost all their defenses against wheat rust. But Borlaug's big success was the introduction of the dwarfing gene from the Japanese *Norin 10* into the Mexican wheat varieties.

Borlaug began increasing wheat yields by dousing the
Mexican wheat plants with nitrogen fertilizer. The problem
was that the higher-yielding plants were so heavy they fell
over before they could be harvested—just as their northern
cousins had done before U.S. breeders had embraced the
dwarfing gene. Borlaug sent for the *Norin 10* dwarf seed and
the problem was solved. The new wheat plants were twenty to
forty inches tall, compared with the fifty to sixty inches for the
traditional varieties. Mexican wheat production soared.

All Mexicans benefited in some way from the sudden
rise in food grain production, but the new package—seed,
fertilizer, and other chemicals needed to produce the new
yields—was too expensive for all but the richest farmers. A
wealthy group of fewer than two hundred millionaire entre-
preneurs established themselves quickly in the forefront of
Mexico's food production. The Mexican government encouraged this elite. The state offered sources of credit for farming
operations and private irrigation schemes, fostered mechaniza-
tion by special exchange rates, and established guaranteed
prices for wheat. By 1951 Borlaug's new wheat varieties were
being grown on 70 percent of the wheat fields. Five years later
Mexico was self-sufficient in wheat. At the same time, wheat
yields of the poorer farmers dragged behind those of the more
prosperous commercial sector.

As a result of helping to set up a Mexican agribusiness,
U.S. seed companies gained long-term access to Mexico's
priceless gene pool of traditional corn varieties. As part of
the Mexican program, the Rockefeller Foundation opened the
International Maize and Wheat Improvement Center, a
research center and collection of genetic information on native

Mexican corn, including a seed bank that would eventually preserve more than one hundred thousand varieties. The seed companies were happy, but the primary purpose of these seed banks was to hold their valuable collections in trust for all humanity.

Similar publicly funded agricultural research centers and associated seed banks were set up in the Philippines for rice, in Colombia for beans, and eventually in Africa for rice, cassava, and maize. By the early 1990s sixteen such centers were spread over five continents, but the African centers still lagged behind the rest of the world because farmers there could derive little benefit from the technical package offered by the West. In some cases the crop was inappropriate, in others the African farmers simply could not afford the chemicals being offered. The research laboratories were all coordinated by the Consultative Group on International Agricultural Research (CGIAR), research centers financed by the advanced industrial nations, private foundations and international regional organizations, the Rockefeller and Ford foundations, and the World Bank. One aim was agricultural, the other geopolitical. "The Green Revolution operated in areas susceptible to communism," concluded a Dutch study. In some accounts, this aspect would obscure the humanitarian mission.

After Mexico, Borlaug and the Rockefeller and Ford-sponsored research teams scored similar successes with wheat and rice programs in Asia, where population was increasing at an alarming rate and traditional farming methods simply could not cope. In the early 1960s the wheat yield in India and China was similar to that of Europe during the

Middle Ages. Famines followed if crops failed. The expansion of farm acreage was reaching the limit of arable land.

The Green Revolutionaries introduced the same three-part package of new varieties, irrigation systems, and chemical fertilizers. Production soared. The 1968 wheat harvest in India was one-third greater than the previous record; schools had to be closed to provide space to store the grain. One study showed that the increase in India's wheat production from the new varieties was so great, another 100 million acres of land would have had to be plowed up to obtain the same yields with old varieties. Worldwide, between 750 and 1,200 million acres would have been needed, according to the study. The new wheat varieties were also popular in Latin American countries.

Again the dwarfing gene was decisive. After the new rice research station started distributing a dwarf rice in the mid-1960s, the Philippines became self-sufficient in rice production for the first time in decades. In Colombia the new rice did so well, it became the country's dominant food crop. In 1970 Borlaug's labors were rewarded with the Nobel Peace Prize; he was the first plant breeder to receive the honor.

Geopolitics apart, an increase in food production was the top priority of these programs, and as a result they saved millions of people from starvation. The statistics are stunning. The total amount of food available per person in the world rose by 11 percent over the two decades of the '70s and '80s, while the estimated number of hungry people fell from 942 million to 786 million, a 16 percent drop.

In the early 1980s "the all clear was sounded, signifying a job well done," as the director of the International Food

Policy Research Institute (part of the CGIAR consortium), Per Pinstrup-Andersen, would put it. But he and others were worried about the fallout from this success. M. S. Swaminathan, the international agronomist and promoter of the Indian Green Revolution, would recall how in the same year, 1968, that the Green Revolution had been given its name, he had warned, "Exploitative agriculture offers great possibilities if carried out in a scientific way, but poses great dangers if carried out with only an immediate profit motive. The emerging exploitative farming community in India should become aware of this. Intensive cultivation of the land without conservation of soil fertility . . . would lead, ultimately, to the springing up of deserts . . . Therefore the initiation of exploitative agriculture without a proper understanding of the various consequences of every one of the changes introduced into traditional agriculture, and without first building up a proper scientific and training base to sustain it, may only lead us, in the long run, into an era of agricultural disaster rather than one of agricultural prosperity." In 1999 Swaminathan observed, "The significance of my 1968 analysis has been widely realized."

The Green Revolution had not brought world hunger under control. Even the doubling of food production would still leave an estimated 800 million "food insecure" in 2025. And while the successes had averted famine for millions and India's granaries might have been overflowing, 5,000 children died in India each day from malnutrition. While increases in the yields of three staple crops—corn, wheat, and rice— helped the poor raise their living standards where those crops are eaten, improvement in African staples, such as cassava, sorghum, and sweet potatoes, received lower priority and became known as "orphan crops."

———□———

In the early 2000s, a new wave of genetically modified crops
arrived called pharmacrops. These new crops are plants modified to provide ingredients for industrial and medical products,
including drugs that could be used to treat or prevent AIDS,
herpes, and cancer.

   Advocates of the technology envision pharmacrops
producing less expensive and more accessible vaccines and
medical treatments. Opponents believe that the dangers of the
technology are significant and far reaching. Corn that has
been genetically engineered to, for example, provide a protein
for a herpes medication is not meant to be eaten and may contain genetic traits that should not be spread to corn that is
sold in supermarkets. Opponents worry that there is no way
to control contamination of non-pharmacrops and argue for
stronger regulation. Some of those calling for greater regulation are major players in the $500 billion food industry.

   In the following article, Lucinda Fleeson, a former
reporter for the Philadelphia Inquirer and currently a professor at the University of Maryland, examines how such
regulation might affect the farmers who are turning to pharmacrops in Iowa's corn belt. —SG

"A Cure for the Common Farm?"
by Lucinda Fleeson
Mother Jones, March/April 2003

From early spring to harvesttime last year, Iowa farmer Bill
Horan watched over a small plot of corn that grew behind an
electric fence, bordered by a moat of fallow earth, a quarter

mile from the next cornfield. The plants in the high-security field had been genetically engineered—not to grow taller or to defeat pests, but to produce a human enzyme, lipase, used in treating cystic fibrosis. And to Horan, a fourth-generation family farmer, those rows of stalks represented the future. "Biotechnology is going to take the plywood down from Main Streets in rural America," he predicted.

"Pharming," the practice of altering corn, tobacco, and other plants to make drugs for humans and animals, has been getting a lot of attention in the biotech industry—and attracting plenty of controversy. Last year, pharmaceutical crops were being grown in some 350 test plots around the nation, and it's estimated that pharming could become a $12 billion industry within the next three years. Researchers and companies say the crops could make drugs cheaper and more available, but critics—including environmentalists and grocery manufacturers—warn that the technology is being rushed to production without sufficient regulation. Caught in the middle are small and midsize farmers, desperate for a crop that could, for the first time in years, help them turn a profit.

Clearly, traditional commodity farming can't save the Corn Belt. As corn and soybean farms have grown, profits have shrunk to the point where most growers are kept afloat only by government subsidies. The landscape near Horan's farm is dotted with empty buildings and ghost towns; in nearby Rockwell City, the self-proclaimed "golden buckle of the Corn Belt," the last new house was built two years ago, and the Presbyterians have had to move in with the Lutherans because they can no longer afford their own church. "No one is making money around here," says Neil

Oswald, a John Deere dealer in nearby Manson, noting that in a good year, farmers can expect to invest $320 an acre for a harvest worth $350 an acre.

By contrast, pharmaceutical crops could fetch yields up to $15,000 an acre—and, Horan notes, these "boutique" crops don't need much space. "Biotech rewards management, not size," he says. "A 500-acre farmer or a 5,000-acre farmer can both play in this game. We don't have to keep making farms bigger and bigger, which means that there are fewer and fewer people supporting our rural churches and schools."

Small farmers may also be better suited than giant agribusinesses to the intensive monitoring pharmacrops require, says Tom Slunecka of the National Corn Growers Association. And it's not just farmers who could benefit, he adds; high-tech processing plants "could be very profitable within rural communities." Right now, Iowa exports college graduates; pharmacrops, Slunecka maintains, could bring some of them back.

For now, most of the new crops are being grown on plots managed by pharmaceutical companies and universities. But for the past eight years, Horan—who, along with his brother, is the first individual grower to hold a U.S. Department of Agriculture permit to grow drugs for humans—has been working to change that. He entered farm politics, became president of the Iowa Corn Growers Association, and assembled a cooperative of fellow Iowa farmers interested in growing pharmacrops. He's traveled to Washington to meet with regulators, and to France to win a contract to grow the lipase corn for the biotech company Meristem. Armed with PowerPoint slides and his just-folks Midwestern drawl, he speaks at conferences of grocery manufacturers and seed companies, arguing that pharmacrops present an opportunity, not a danger, for the nation's breadbasket.

At dusk on a chilly October day, Bill Horan drove his "cowboy Cadillac," a big, red Chevy pickup, to a spot 1,300 feet away from his one-acre lipase plot; outsiders were allowed no closer. The corn was surrounded by 100 feet of bare earth and lay in the midst of 440 acres of soybean fields. To prevent pollen drift, the corn had been bred to be sterile; for extra protection it was planted six weeks after the other corn in the state had pollinated. In a few days, Horan would harvest the crop with a special combine and transport it to a locked barn, burning any discarded material and plowing over the test plot to bury any dropped kernels. Come spring, he said, he'll go back and spray any stray sprouts with Roundup.

There is good reason for all those protections. Last fall, the pharmacrop industry's worst nightmare came true when an ounce of pharmaceutical corn was found mixed with soybeans in an Aurora, Nebraska, grain elevator. ProdiGene Inc., the company that owned the escaped corn, was ordered by the USDA to destroy 500,000 bushels of soybeans and pay a $250,000 fine for violating safety procedures. The incident amplified concerns that with "just one mistake by a biotech company, we'll be eating other people's prescription drugs in our cornflakes," as Larry Bohlen of Friends of the Earth puts it. A report from the Genetically Engineered Food Alert, a coalition skeptical of biotechnology, warns that pharmaceuticals could leach into the soil through plant roots, that sterility measures could fail, or that new genes could add unexpected traits to the crops, turning them into superweeds. Secretary of Agriculture Ann Veneman said in December that she will consider tougher rules on pharmacrops; critics are urging regulators to confine the plants to enclosed greenhouses.

In farm states, the pharmacrop debate has become a major political issue. Last fall, the Biotechnology Industry Organization declared a voluntary moratorium on growing pharmaceuticals in the Corn Belt, then quickly reversed its position after protests from Iowa's two senators and its governor. Iowa State University's Research Park plans to build a $15 million facility to extract proteins from genetically modified material; similar efforts are being mounted in Minnesota, California, and other states. "We simply can't wait until all the questions are answered and all the development work is done," says Steven Carter, president of Iowa State's research park, "or all the biotech facilities are likely to end up on the coasts."

Still, there are concerns that pharmacrops could have a boomerang effect. Growers could be found liable for transgenic pollen drift to neighbors' farms, warns the trade group American Corn Growers Association, and fear of genetically engineered food still prevails in Japan and Europe. Grain handlers, grocery manufacturers, and food processors "are all saying this is a new technology and they're just not comfortable with it," acknowledges Lisa Dry of the Biotechnology Industry Organization. "It's not agriculture. It's pharmaceutical production."

In early December, a Meristem official from France visited Horan's farm for a top-to-bottom inspection as the company pondered whether to increase his contract to 25 acres, a level nearly sufficient for commercial production of the drug. The inspector, Laure Brien, gave the farm her highest marks. "Everything they did was perfectly done," she says.

But perfect just might not be good enough.

———◼———

In 1999, a new rice plant was invented through the joint efforts of scientists Dr. Ingo Potrykus of the Swiss Federal Institute of Technology and Dr. Peter Beyer of the University of Freiburg in Germany. This "golden" rice, its rich color the result of the high amounts of beta-carotene it contained, was quickly publicized as a savior of citizens of third-world countries.

Soon, however, unforeseen issues arose. Many of these issues were not concerns over safety or effectiveness of this new food, but instead dealt with more practical and political problems. A central problem was how to get the rice to the people who needed it. Another issue was the large public response to this crop as another instance of the Western world, from which the crops came, imposing its ideas and power on the citizens of developing countries. Would these crops damage third-world farmland and leave citizens dependent on food grown outside their countries? In the following article, J. Madeleine Nash explores the implications, sense of hope, fears, and disappointment that golden rice has produced in its first five years of existence. —SG

"Grains of Hope"
by J. Madeleine Nash
Time, July 31, 2000

At first, the grains of rice that Ingo Potrykus sifted through his fingers did not seem at all special, but that was because they were still encased in their dark, crinkly husks. Once those drab coverings were stripped away and the interiors polished to a glossy sheen, Potrykus and his colleagues would behold the seeds' golden secret. At their core, these grains were not pearly white, as ordinary rice is, but a very pale yellow—courtesy of beta-carotene, the nutrient that serves as a building block for vitamin A.

Potrykus was elated. For more than a decade he had dreamed of creating such a rice: a golden rice that would improve the lives of millions of the poorest people in the world. He'd visualized peasant farmers wading into paddies to set out the tender seedlings and winnowing the grain at harvest time in handwoven baskets. He'd pictured small children consuming the golden gruel their mothers would make, knowing that it would sharpen their eyesight and strengthen their resistance to infectious diseases.

And he saw his rice as the first modest start of a new green revolution, in which ancient food crops would acquire all manner of useful properties: bananas that wouldn't rot on the way to market; corn that could supply its own fertilizer; wheat that could thrive in drought-ridden soil.

But imagining a golden rice, Potrykus soon found, was one thing and bringing one into existence quite another. Year after year, he and his colleagues ran into one unexpected obstacle after another, beginning with the finicky growing habits of the rice they transplanted to a greenhouse near the foothills of the Swiss Alps. When success finally came, in the spring of 1999, Potrykus was 65 and about to retire as a full professor at the Swiss Federal Institute of Technology in Zurich. At that point, he tackled an even more formidable challenge.

Having created golden rice, Potrykus wanted to make sure it reached those for whom it was intended: malnourished children of the developing world. And that, he knew, was not likely to be easy. Why? Because in addition to a full complement of genes from *Oryza sativa*—the Latin name for the most commonly consumed species of rice—the golden grains also contained snippets of DNA borrowed from bacteria and daffodils. It was what some would call Frankenfood, a product of genetic engineering. As such, it was entangled in a web of hopes and fears and political baggage, not to mention a fistful of ironclad patents.

For about a year now—ever since Potrykus and his chief collaborator, Peter Beyer of the University of Freiburg in Germany, announced their achievement—their golden grain has illuminated an increasingly polarized public debate. At issue is the question of what genetically engineered crops represent. Are they, as their proponents argue, a technological leap forward that will bestow incalculable benefits on the world and its people? Or do they represent a perilous step down a slippery slope that will lead to ecological and agricultural ruin? Is genetic engineering just a more efficient way to do the business of conventional crossbreeding? Or does the ability to mix the genes of any species—even plants and animals—give man more power than he should have?

The debate erupted the moment genetically engineered crops made their commercial debut in the mid-1990s, and it has escalated ever since. First to launch major protests against biotechnology were European environmentalists and consumer-advocacy groups. They were soon followed by their

U.S. counterparts, who made a big splash at last fall's World Trade Organization meeting in Seattle and last week launched an offensive designed to target one company after another. Over the coming months, charges that transgenic crops pose grave dangers will be raised in petitions, editorials, mass mailings and protest marches. As a result, golden rice, despite its humanitarian intent, will probably be subjected to the same kind of hostile scrutiny that has already led to curbs on the commercialization of these crops in Britain, Germany, Switzerland and Brazil.

The hostility is understandable. Most of the genetically engineered crops introduced so far represent minor variations on the same two themes: resistance to insect pests and to herbicides used to control the growth of weeds. And they are often marketed by large, multinational corporations that produce and sell the very agricultural chemicals farmers are spraying on their fields. So while many farmers have embraced such crops as Monsanto's Roundup Ready soybeans, with their genetically engineered resistance to Monsanto's Roundup-brand herbicide, that let them spray weed killer without harming crops, consumers have come to regard such things with mounting suspicion. Why resort to a strange new technology that might harm the biosphere, they ask, when the benefits of doing so seem small?

Indeed, the benefits have seemed small—until golden rice came along to suggest otherwise. Golden rice is clearly not the moral equivalent of Roundup Ready beans. Quite the contrary, it is an example—the first compelling example—of a genetically engineered crop that may benefit not just the farmers who grow it but also the consumers who eat it. In this

case, the consumers include at least a million children who die
every year because they are weakened by vitamin-A deficiency
and an additional 350,000 who go blind.

No wonder the biotech industry sees golden rice as a
powerful ally in its struggle to win public acceptance. No wonder its critics see it as a cynical ploy. And no wonder so many
of those concerned about the twin evils of poverty and hunger
look at golden rice and see reflected in it their own passionate
conviction that genetically engineered crops can be made to
serve the greater public good—that in fact such crops have a
critical role to play in feeding a world that is about to add to
its present population of 6 billion. As former President Jimmy
Carter put it, "Responsible biotechnology is not the enemy;
starvation is."

Indeed, by the year 2020, the demand for grain, both for
human consumption and for animal feed, is projected to go up
by nearly half, while the amount of arable land available to
satisfy that demand will not only grow much more slowly but
also, in some areas, will probably dwindle. Add to that the
need to conserve overstressed water resources and reduce the
use of polluting chemicals, and the enormity of the challenge
becomes apparent. In order to meet it, believes Gordon
Conway, the agricultural ecologist who heads the Rockefeller
Foundation, 21st century farmers will have to draw on every
arrow in their agricultural quiver, including genetic engineering. And contrary to public perception, he says, those who
have the least to lose and the most to gain are not well-fed
Americans and Europeans but the hollow-bellied citizens of
the developing world.

Going for the Gold

It was in the late 1980s, after he became a full professor of plant science at the Swiss Federal Institute of Technology, that Ingo Potrykus started to think about using genetic engineering to improve the nutritional qualities of rice. He knew that of some 3 billion people who depend on rice as their major staple, around 10% risk some degree of vitamin-A deficiency and the health problems that result. The reason, some alleged, was an overreliance on rice ushered in by the green revolution. Whatever its cause, the result was distressing: these people were so poor that they ate a few bowls of rice a day and almost nothing more.

The problem interested Potrykus for a number of reasons. For starters, he was attracted by the scientific challenge of transferring not just a single gene, as many had already done, but a group of genes that represented a key part of a biochemical pathway. He was also motivated by complex emotions, among them empathy. Potrykus knew more than most what it meant not to have enough to eat. As a child growing up in war-ravaged Germany, he and his brothers were often so desperately hungry that they ate what they could steal.

Around 1990, Potrykus hooked up with Gary Toenniessen, director of food security for the Rockefeller Foundation. Toenniessen had identified the lack of beta-carotene in polished rice grains as an appropriate target for gene scientists like Potrykus to tackle because it lay beyond the ability of traditional plant breeding to address. For while rice, like other green plants, contains light-trapping beta-carotene in its external tissues, no plant in the entire *Oryza* genus—as far as anyone knew—produced beta-carotene in its endosperm (the starchy interior part of the rice grain that is all most people eat).

It was at a Rockefeller-sponsored meeting that Potrykus met the University of Freiburg's Peter Beyer, an expert on the beta-carotene pathway in daffodils. By combining their expertise, the two scientists figured, they might be able to remedy this unfortunate oversight in nature. So in 1993, with some $100,000 in seed money from the Rockefeller Foundation, Potrykus and Beyer launched what turned into a seven-year, $2.6 million project, backed also by the Swiss government and the European Union. "I was in a privileged situation," reflects Potrykus, "because I was able to operate without industrial support. Only in that situation can you think of giving away your work free."

That indeed is what Potrykus announced he and Beyer planned to do. The two scientists soon discovered, however, that giving away golden rice was not going to be as easy as they thought. The genes they transferred and the bacteria they used to transfer those genes were all encumbered by patents and proprietary rights. Three months ago, the two scientists struck a deal with AstraZeneca, which is based in London and holds an exclusive license to one of the genes Potrykus and Beyer used to create golden rice. In exchange for commercial marketing rights in the U.S. and other affluent markets, AstraZeneca agreed to lend its financial muscle and legal expertise to the cause of putting the seeds into the hands of poor farmers at no charge.

No sooner had the deal been made than the critics of agricultural biotechnology erupted. "A rip-off of the public trust," grumbled the Rural Advancement Foundation International, an advocacy group based in Winnipeg, Canada. "Asian farmers get (unproved) genetically modified rice, and AstraZeneca gets the 'gold.'" Potrykus was dismayed by such negative reaction. "It would be irresponsible," he exclaimed, "not to say immoral, not to use biotechnology to try to solve this problem!" But such expressions of good intentions would not be enough to allay his opponents' fears.

Weighing the Perils

Beneath the hyperbolic talk of Frankenfoods and Superweeds, even proponents of agricultural biotechnology agree, lie a number of real concerns. To begin with, all foods, including the transgenic foods created through genetic engineering, are potential sources of allergens. That's because the transferred genes contain instructions for making proteins, and not all proteins are equal. Some—those in peanuts, for example—are well known for causing allergic reactions. To many, the possibility that golden rice might cause such a problem seems farfetched, but it nonetheless needs to be considered.

Then there is the problem of "genetic pollution," as opponents of biotechnology term it. Pollen grains from such wind-pollinated plants as corn and canola, for instance, are carried far and wide. To farmers, this mainly poses a nuisance. Transgenic canola grown in one field, for example, can very easily pollinate nontransgenic plants grown in the next. Indeed this is the reason behind the furor that recently erupted in Europe when it was discovered that canola seeds from Canada—unwittingly planted by farmers in England, France, Germany and Sweden—contained transgenic contaminants.

The continuing flap over Bt corn and cotton—now grown not only in the U.S. but also in Argentina and China—has provided more fodder for debate. Bt stands for a common soil bacteria, *Bacillus thuringiensis*, different strains of which produce toxins that target specific insects. By transferring to corn and cotton the bacterial gene responsible for making this toxin, Monsanto and other companies have produced crops that are resistant to the European corn borer and the cotton bollworm. An immediate concern, raised by a number of ecologists, is whether or not widespread planting of these crops will spur the development of resistance to Bt among crop pests. That would be unfortunate, they point out, because Bt is a safe and effective natural insecticide that is popular with organic farmers.

Even more worrisome are ecological concerns. In 1999 Cornell University entomologist John Losey performed a provocative, "seat-of-the-pants" laboratory experiment. He dusted Bt corn pollen on plants populated by monarch-butterfly caterpillars. Many of the caterpillars died. Could what happened in Losey's laboratory happen in cornfields across the Midwest? Were these lovely butterflies, already under pressure owing to human encroachment on their Mexican wintering grounds, about to face a new threat from high-tech farmers in the north?

The upshot: despite studies pro and con—and countless save-the-monarch protests acted out by children dressed in butterfly costumes—a conclusive answer to this question has yet to come. Losey himself is not yet convinced that Bt corn poses a grave danger to North America's monarch-butterfly population, but he does think the issue deserves attention. And others agree. "I'm not anti biotechnology per se," says biologist Rebecca Goldberg, a senior scientist with the Environmental Defense Fund, "but I would like to have a tougher regulatory regime. These crops should be subject to more careful screening before they are released."

Are there more potential pitfalls? There are. Among other things, there is the possibility that as transgenes in pollen drift, they will fertilize wild plants, and weeds will emerge that are hardier and even more difficult to control. No one knows how common the exchange of genes between domestic plants and their wild relatives really is, but Margaret Mellon, director of the Union of Concerned Scientists' agriculture and biotechnology program, is certainly not alone in thinking that it's high time we find out. Says she: "People should be responding to these concerns with experiments, not assurances."

And that is beginning to happen, although—contrary to expectations—the reports coming in are not necessarily that scary. For three years now, University of Arizona entomologist Bruce Tabashnik has been monitoring fields of Bt cotton that farmers have planted in his state. And in this instance at least, he says, "the environmental risks seem minimal, and the benefits seem great." First of all, cotton is self-pollinated rather than wind-pollinated, so that the spread of the Bt gene is of less concern. And because the Bt gene is so effective, he notes, Arizona farmers have reduced their use of chemical insecticides 75%. So far, the pink bollworm population has not rebounded, indicating that the feared resistance to Bt has not yet developed.

Assessing the Promise

Are the critics of agricultural biotechnology right? Is biotech's promise nothing more than overblown corporate hype? The papaya growers in Hawaii's Puna district clamor to disagree. In 1992 a wildfire epidemic of papaya ringspot virus threatened to destroy the state's papaya industry; by 1994, nearly half the state's papaya acreage had been infected, their owners forced to seek outside employment. But then help arrived, in the form of a virus-resistant transgenic papaya developed by Cornell University plant pathologist Dennis Gonsalves.

In 1995 a team of scientists set up a field trial of two transgenic lines—UH SunUP and UH Rainbow—and by 1996, the verdict had been rendered. As everyone could see, the non-transgenic plants in the field trial were a stunted mess, and the transgenic plants were healthy. In 1998, after negotiations with four patent holders, the papaya growers switched en masse to the transgenic seeds and reclaimed their orchards. "Consumer acceptance has been great," reports Rusty Perry, who runs a papaya farm near Puna. "We've found that customers are more concerned with how the fruits look and taste than with whether they are transgenic or not."

Viral diseases, along with insect infestations, are a major cause of crop loss in Africa, observes Kenyan plant scientist Florence Wambugu. African sweet-potato fields, for example, yield only 2.4 tons per acre, vs. more than double that in the rest of the world. Soon Wambugu hopes to start raising those yields by introducing a transgenic sweet potato that is resistant to the feathery mottle virus. There really is no other option, explains Wambugu, who currently directs the International

Service for the Acquisition of Agri-biotech Applications in Nairobi. "You can't control the virus in the field, and you can't breed in resistance through conventional means."

To Wambugu, the flap in the U.S. and Europe over genetically engineered crops seems almost ludicrous. In Africa, she notes, nearly half the fruit and vegetable harvest is lost because it rots on the way to market. "If we had a transgenic banana that ripened more slowly," she says, "we could have 40% more bananas than now." Wambugu also dreams of getting access to herbicide-resistant crops. Says she: "We could liberate so many people if our crops were resistant to herbicides that we could then spray on the surrounding weeds. Weeding enslaves Africans; it keeps children from school."

In Wambugu's view, there are more benefits to be derived from agricultural biotechnology in Africa than practically anywhere else on the planet—and this may be so. Among the genetic-engineering projects funded by the Rockefeller Foundation is one aimed at controlling striga, a weed that parasitizes the roots of African corn plants. At present there is little farmers can do about striga infestation, so tightly intertwined are the weed's roots with the roots of the corn plants it targets. But scientists have come to understand the source of the problem: corn roots exude chemicals that attract striga. So it may prove possible to identify the genes that are responsible and turn them off.

The widespread perception that agricultural biotechnology is intrinsically inimical to the environment perplexes the Rockefeller Foundation's Conway, who views genetic engineering as an important tool for achieving what he has termed a "doubly green revolution." If the technology can marshal a plant's natural defenses against weeds and viruses, if it can induce crops to flourish with minimal application of chemical fertilizers, if it can make dryland agriculture more productive without straining local water supplies, then what's wrong with it?

Of course, these particular breakthroughs have not happened yet. But as the genomes of major crops are ever more finely mapped, and as the tools for transferring genes become ever more precise, the possibility for tinkering with complex biochemical pathways can be expected to expand rapidly. As Potrykus sees it, there is no question that agricultural biotechnology can be harnessed for the good of humankind. The only question is whether there is the collective will to do so. And the answer may well emerge as the people of the world weigh the future of golden rice.

CHAPTER THREE

PRODUCTION, DISTRIBUTION, AND CONSUMPTION: THE IMPACT OF GM FOODS

There is quite a lot of controversy concerning genetically modified foods. In essence, the controversy can be summarized as the complex struggle between different forces in politics, science, social policy, and economics. When one gets caught up in the debate, it is easy to forget about one very important and basic aspect. What we are talking about, after all is said and done, is food. William Woys Weaver, a prolific food writer and food historian, sees food as an integral part of our culture. When farmers are forced, through economic and other pressures, to plant more profitable GM crops, other varieties of that crop are threatened with extinction. In Weaver's opinion, this is a great tragedy, for when a crop (and its seeds) become extinct, parts of human culture and history are lost with them.

In the following article, author and educator John Feffer reports on Weaver's far-reaching efforts to save seeds from extinction. The article originally appeared at AlterNet.org, an online news site that has won numerous awards, including the Independent Press Award for Online Political Coverage —SG

"The World in a Seed"
by John Feffer
AlterNet.org, September 25, 2004

William Woys Weaver is the horticultural equivalent of the book memorizers of "Fahrenheit 451." The characters of Ray Bradbury's novel seared the texts of forbidden books into their memories to save them from the fires of a police state. William Weaver and his fellow seed savers are preserving fruits and vegetables against the homogenizing pressures of agribusiness.

"Seeds represent entire civilizations, miniaturized to fit into the palm of our hand," he says. When a venerable seed variety perishes, as with the loss of a valuable manuscript, human culture dies by degrees.

One of America's foremost food historians, Weaver lives in a partially restored 1805 inn on what once was the main route between Philadelphia and Lancaster, Pennsylvania. Along one side of his house is an English garden. In the back are pots containing a fruit paradise of quinces, medlars, lemons, pomegranates, citrons, even a limequat that apparently makes a mean marmalade. Down a slope from the front of the house, however, is the real treasure; a succession of raised beds containing a colorful riot of vegetables and flowers.

"It's a seed garden," Weaver explains without a hint of apology in his voice, "not a Martha-Stewart-kind-of-beautiful garden."

Different varieties are placed in such a way as to diminish the likelihood of unintended cross-breeding and to ensure that the subsequent seeds will yield predictable results.

The garden is rich in both history and geography. Weaver shows me a white ovoid vegetable: the original eggplant brought from India to England where it received its English name. I try a citrus-accented ground cherry that comes in its own papery wrapper. There's a little purple potato from Switzerland, a sprawling cardoon of Tours, his own breeds of tomatoes and dahlias. Colonial Williamsburg and other historical recreations routinely hit up Weaver for authentic produce of the period, such as an 18th-century squash grown from seeds passed down by a Delaware community descended from the Nannacoke Indians.

In one corner of the garden grows an Ole Pepperpot pepper, the seeds of which he found preserved in a baby food jar in the bottom of his grandmother's deep freezer. In the 19th century, the African-American community used this pepper to create pepperpot soup, a Philadelphia-area specialty. Weaver's grandfather received the seeds from his friend Horace Pippin, the great African-American painter, and today the variety flourishes in Weaver's garden. "If I could only find the portrait Pippin did of my father," he says, "I could finally restore my kitchen."

Because of the large investments of labor and money, it is "probably the most expensive garden in Pennsylvania," Weaver laments. "I used to complain to my grandmother about the cost of the garden. And she said, 'why are you doing it?' 'I like the garden,' I said. So she said, 'Just take the money out of the equation then.'"

The seed garden's diversity and sense of history mirrors Weaver's wide-ranging professional interests. Encouraged to write by Alexandra Tolstoy, the daughter of the great Russian novelist, Weaver went on to study international relations and architecture before seizing on food writing to pay the bills. He is the author of definitive books on scrapple, American food ways, Pennsylvania Dutch and Quaker cooking.

Jane Lear of *Gourmet* magazine, where Weaver is a contributing editor, likens him to a culinary Google—"an invaluable resource of information" whether providing information on heirloom vegetables or, for a *Gourmet* article on artichokes, the intriguing scrap of information that Marilyn Monroe was once crowned artichoke queen of 1948. Weaver has a novelist's flair for capturing the flavor and drama of food. "He's describing these tomatoes and you just want to rip them off the page and eat them," Lear says.

Weaver's life work is an example of connectedness, a term he uses in his book "America Eats" (1989) to describe the intricate relationships between growers, cooks and communities. Each of his projects somehow connects to his own genealogy. His books on Pennsylvania Dutch and Quaker cooking celebrate that part of his family that has lived in Pennsylvania for at least 13 generations. His annotations of a book on Polish medieval cooking connect to his Polish side, represented by his middle name, Woys. And his work on seeds is a direct continuation of his grandfather's seed-saving efforts.

"When I first got into my grandfather's collection, I didn't know what I was doing," he tells me as we tour the gardens, which were re-created according to their original 1830s design. "This survived the first round of ignorance."

Much of Weaver's writing is devoted to the context in which food is grown and eaten, so he is particularly attuned to political contexts. He has written about the boycott recipes of 19th-century American abolitionists who refused to use ingredients produced by slave labor; the challenges of writing about Polish national cuisine in a Marxist country; and the nonviolent approach to nature of the Quakers. His approach to food, like that of MFK Fisher before him, embodies a culinary ecology whereby nothing edible is wasted, which in part explains his fondness for the sausage-like scrapple. But much of his writing inevitably returns to that essential kernel of truth: the seed.

Seeds, like books, are repositories of information. They contain important genetic material that can replenish stocks damaged by disease. When blight hit the U.S. corn crop in the 1970s, genes from a disease-resistant wild variety of maize in Mexico, which was incidentally down to its last 25 acres of habitat, saved the day. The Irish, as Weaver writes in "100 Vegetables and Where They Came From," were not so fortunate when blight ravaged field after field of lumper potatoes in the 1840s.

Fruit and vegetable varieties are rapidly disappearing and not simply through changes in taste or fashion. As part of its efforts to standardize trade, the European Union has outlawed the sale of thousands of heirloom varieties. Agribusiness supports monocropping to maximize efficiency. Biotechnology firms are patenting new genetically modified seeds that may well threaten older varieties through unintended crossbreeding. And seed companies are downsizing their catalogs to save money.

Four years ago, the seed company Seminis eliminated 2,000 varieties from its catalog. As Cary Fowler and Pat

Mooney relate in their book on seed politics, "Shattering," nearly 90 percent of the varieties of pears and apples once grown in the United States in the 19th century are now extinct.

Weaver expresses concern about the Russet potato monoculture of McDonald's and the way Chardonnay is replacing many unusual grape varieties across Europe. It's not exactly the police state of "Fahrenheit 451," but the sheer loss of information contained in the lost seed varieties is staggering.

Inside his kitchen, as he chops green tomatoes, peppers and carrots for a Pennsylvania Dutch–style pickalilly and we sip a slightly fermented lemonade kefir with fig flavors, Weaver tells cautionary tales about seeds. He recently bought some kohlrabi seeds at a local store, and with a little sleuthing, traced the chain of ownership from the name on the packet (Miracle Grow) to the parent company (Scott) and from there to the shadowy corporations OMS Investments and Delaware Corporate Management. This is a far cry from the farmer who carefully saves seeds from one harvest to the next, strengthening ties of stewardship rather than ownership.

"We're collapsing the ownership of the land into the hands of very few people," Weaver tells me. "We're indenturing farmers in a very different way. Farmers are now indentured to the land and the bankers own the ground."

This has reduced farmers to little more than modern-day serfs or, as Weaver says, "facilitators of technologies owned by a third party," and "the ownership of seed makes it more absolute."

Farmers are dependent on large seed companies for the latest varieties of hybrid seeds, the fertilizer and pesticides that work best with them, and even the specialized machinery to harvest the crops. Five companies control 75 percent of the global vegetable seed market, according to Helena Paul and Ricarda Steinbrecher's "Hungry Corporations," and this concentration of the marketplace threatens global genetic diversity.

The new patterns of ownership add up to what Weaver calls the "new feudalism." Genetically modified seeds, because they preclude seed saving and threaten to contaminate conventional stocks, are only a new variation on an old theme.

"GMO and patented crops have shifted the economic risk to the farmer. This was like the Middle Ages when all the economic risk was shifted onto the serf," Weaver says. "It doesn't matter to Monsanto if the GM fails. You bought it. It's your problem if it fails."

In opposition to this corporate control over farmers, Weaver has emphasized "connectedness." Seeds provide one means of connecting to history and culture. Seedsaving, too, brings people together, not in a spatially defined community but in one of affinity, knitting organizations like Seed Savers Exchange in Iowa and Kokopelli in France to thousands of individual gardeners and farmers.

Seed savers range "from anarchists to the person who found Jesus in the garden," Weaver says. "The country is so divided now and this brings people together and we realize we have a common goal."

He's quick to qualify his idea. "You can get too romantic about connectedness, too gooey and touchy-feely," he says. And he points to his latest focus of research: Cyprus. Weaver hopes that through his ethnographic research and sifting of archaeological evidence, he will help to rewrite the history of the Middle Ages when Cyprus served as a key source and conduit of food ways to Europe.

"Cyprus is the ultimate break—no connectedness, no genealogical link. It's a liberating topic." And yet, Cyprus appeals precisely because it connects to many of his preoccupations as a food historian. When he's doing his research, he says, "I feel like I'm up on some elevated platform and I'm looking down on the whole Eastern Mediterranean and seeing all these connections."

I am eager to hear more about his latest research in Cyprus, but I also don't want to inadvertently poach the new material. "The more people talk about Cyprus the better," he reassures me. Weaver is as generous with information as he is with his seeds. He makes the point explicitly with a horticultural example—the dependency of corn on human propagation.

"People didn't sit on the corn," he says. "They traded it around. They shared the seed."

———■———

The debate over the labeling of genetically modified foods seems unlikely to end any time soon. Some strongly believe in government-enforced, mandatory labeling of all consumer products. Another camp believes that consumers pay little attention to labeling or often do not understand the jargon. Another group believes that labeling may deter people from buying products that are genetically engineered to be beneficial to them. Others believe that better regulation of the production of GM foods, not food labels, is the only real guarantee of safety. In part, this diversity of opinion is a result of consumers not being able to see the dangers or benefits of these foods borne out, as it remains too early to observe any long-term effects of eating and growing genetically modified foods.

In the following article, Jane E. Brody, a personal health columnist for the New York Times, *offers her informed opinion on the important issues, including food labeling, of the GM debate. —SG*

"Facing Biotech Foods Without the Fear Factor"
by Jane E. Brody
New York Times, January 11, 2005

Almost everywhere food is sold these days, you are likely to find products claiming to contain no genetically modified substances. But unless you are buying wild mushrooms, game, berries or fish, that statement is untrue.

Nearly every food we eat has been genetically modified, through centuries of crosses, both within and between species, and for most of the last century through mutations induced by bombarding seeds with chemicals or radiation. In each of these techniques, dozens, hundreds, even thousands of genes of unknown function are transferred or modified to produce new food varieties.

Most so-called organic foods are no exception. The claims of no genetic modification really refer to foods that contain no ingredients that are produced through the highly refined technique of gene splicing, in which one or a few genes are transferred to an organism. But alarmist warnings about the possible hazards of gene splicing have made the public extremely wary of this selective form of genetic modification.

Such warnings have so far been groundless. "Americans have consumed more than a trillion servings of foods that contain gene-spliced ingredients," said Dr. Henry I. Miller, a fellow at the Hoover Institution and author, with Gregory Conko, of "The Frankenfood Myth," a new book that questions the wisdom of current gene-splicing regulations.

"There hasn't been a single untoward event documented, not a single ecosystem disrupted or person made ill from these foods," he said in an interview. "That is not something that can be said about conventional foods, where imprecise methods of genetic modification actually have caused illnesses and deaths."

Ignorance Vs. Progress

It is no secret that the public's understanding of science, and genetics in particular, is low. For example, in a telephone survey of 1,200 Americans released last October by the Food Policy Institute at Rutgers University, 43 percent thought, incorrectly, that ordinary tomatoes did not contain genes, while genetically modified tomatoes did. One-third thought, again incorrectly, that eating genetically modified fruit would change their own genes.

In another telephone survey, in which 1,000 American consumers were questioned last year in research for the Pew Initiative on Food and Biotechnology, 54 percent said they knew little or nothing about genetically modified foods. Still, 89 percent said that no such food should be allowed on the market until the Food and Drug Administration determined that it was safe.

What most respondents did not seem to know is that almost none of the foods people eat every day, which contain many introduced genes whose functions are unknown, have ever been subjected to premarketing approval or postmarketing surveillance.

Why should people object to the presence of a single new gene whose function is known when for centuries they have accepted foods containing hundreds of new genes of unknown function?

A junior high school student in Idaho, Nathan Zohner, demonstrated in a 1997 science fair project how easy it was to hoodwink a scientifically uninformed public. As described in "The Frankenfood Myth," 86 percent of the 50 students he surveyed thought dihydrogen monoxide should be banned after they were told that prolonged exposure to its solid form caused severe tissue damage, that exposure to its gaseous form caused severe burns and that it had been found in tumors from terminal cancer patients. Only one student recognized the substance as water, H_2O.

Without better public understanding and changes in the many arcane rules now thwarting development of new gene-spliced products, we will miss out on major improvements that can result in more healthful foods, a cleaner environment and a worldwide ability to produce more food on less land—using less water, fewer chemicals and less money.

The European Union has, in effect, banned imports of all foods produced through gene splicing, and it has kept many African nations, including those afflicted with widespread malnutrition, from accepting even donated gene-spliced foods and crops by threatening to cut off products they export because they might become contaminated with introduced genes.

Even more puzzling, Uganda has prohibited the testing of a fungus-resistant banana created through gene splicing, even though the fungus is devastating that nation's most important crop.

A Continuum of Techniques

In a new report, "Safety of Genetically Engineered Foods," published by the National Academy of Sciences, an expert committee notes that any time genes are mutated or combined, as occurs in almost all breeding methods, there is a possibility of producing a new, potentially hazardous substance.

Citing a conventionally bred potato that turned out to contain an unintended toxin, the report says the hazard lies with the toxin's presence, not the breeding method.

Among the foods developed through induced mutations are lettuce, beans, grapefruit, rice, oats and wheat. None had to undergo stringent testing and federal approval before reaching the market.

Only those foods produced by the specific introduction of one or more genes into the organism's DNA are subject to strict and prolonged premarketing regulations. But as the academy's report points out, gene splicing is only a process, not a product, a process on a continuum of genetic modification of foods that began more than 10,000 years ago when people first crossed two varieties of a crop to improve its characteristics.

In fact, gene splicing is the most refined, precise and predictable method of genetic modification because the function of the transferred gene or genes is known. It is also important to realize that genes are rarely unique to a given organism.

Regulate by Degree of Risk

All new crop varieties, whether produced through gene splicing or conventional techniques like cross-breeding or induced mutations, go through a series of tests before commercial introduction. After greenhouse testing for the look and perhaps taste of the crop, it is grown in a small, sequestered field trial and, if it passes that test, in a larger trial to check its commercial viability.

The potential risks associated with genetically modified foods result not so much from the method used to produce them but from the traits being introduced. With gene splicing, only one or two traits at a time are introduced, making it possible to assess beforehand how much testing is needed to assure safety.

While such safety tests are important, it is possible to become fixated on hypothetical risks that can never be absolutely discounted.

Indeed, Dr. Miller, once director of the Office of Biotechnology for the Food and Drug Administration, argues that overly stringent regulations can needlessly raise public fears. "People naturally assume that something that is more highly regulated is more dangerous," he said, adding, "Government officials should have done less regulating and more educating."

A risk-based protocol for safety evaluation would greatly reduce the time and costs involved in developing most new gene-spliced crops, many of which could raise the standard of living worldwide and better protect the planet from chemical contamination.

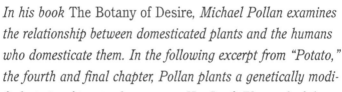

In his book The Botany of Desire, *Michael Pollan examines the relationship between domesticated plants and the humans who domesticate them. In the following excerpt from "Potato," the fourth and final chapter, Pollan plants a genetically modified strain of potato, known as a NewLeaf. The goal of the experiment is to see if the potato will have any adverse effect on his garden. He also simply wants to learn more about GM foods, a subject that to many, including the author, has been shrouded in mystery.*

Pollan's personal journey includes quiet and contemplative moments as he tends to his plants and wonders about their effect on the rest of the garden. His journey also includes a trip to the Monsanto headquarters to learn more about the company that created the NewLeaf potatoes. Pollan's observations raise important questions about nature and GM foods, while leaving the questions tantalizingly unresolved—an appropriate reflection of the issues that surround these controversial crops. —SG

From *The Botany of Desire: A Plant's-Eye View of the World*
by Michael Pollan
2001

It's probably not too much to say that this new technology represents the biggest change in the terms of our relationship with plants since people first learned how to cross one plant with another. With genetic engineering, human control of nature is taking a giant step forward. The kind of reordering of nature represented by the rows in a farmer's field can now take place at a whole new level: within the genome of the plants themselves. Truly, we have stepped out onto new ground.

Or have we?

Just how novel these plants really are is in fact one of the biggest questions about them, and the companies that have developed them give contradictory answers. The industry simultaneously depicts these plants as the linchpins of a biological revolution—part of a "paradigm shift" that will make agriculture more sustainable and feed the world—and, oddly enough, as the same old spuds, corn, and soybeans, at least so far as those of us at the eating end of the food chain should be concerned. The new plants are novel enough to be patented, yet not so novel as to warrant a label telling us what it is we're eating. It would seem they are chimeras: "revolutionary" in the patent office and on the farm, "nothing new" in the supermarket and the environment.

By planting my own crop of NewLeafs, I was hoping to figure out which version of reality to believe, whether these were indeed the same old spuds or something sufficiently novel (in nature, in the diet) to warrant caution and hard questions. As soon as you start looking into the subject, you find that there are many questions about genetically modified plants that, fifty million acres later; remain unanswered and, more remarkable still, unasked-enough to make me think mine might not be the only experiment going on.

May 2. Here at the planter's end of the food chain, where I began my experiment after Monsanto agreed to let me test-drive its NewLeafs, things certainly look new and different. After digging two shallow trenches in my vegetable garden and lining them with compost, I untied the purple mesh bag of seed potatoes Monsanto had sent and opened the grower's guide tied around its neck. Potatoes, you will recall from kindergarten experiments, are grown not from actual seeds but from the eyes of other potatoes, and the dusty, stone-colored chunks of tuber I carefully laid at the bottom of the trench looked much like any other. Yet the grower's guide that comes with them put me in mind not so much of planting vegetables as booting up a new software release.

By "opening and using this product," the card informed me, I was now "licensed" to grow these potatoes, but only for a single generation; the crop I would water and tend and harvest was mine, yet also not mine. That is, the potatoes I would dig come September would be mine to eat or sell, but their genes would remain the intellectual property of Monsanto, protected under several U.S. patents, including 5,196,525; 5,164,316; 5,322,938; and 5,352,605. Were I to save even one of these spuds to plant next year—something I've routinely done with my potatoes in the past—I would be breaking federal law. (I had to wonder, what would be the legal status of any "volunteers"—those plants that, with no prompting from the gardener; sprout each spring from tubers overlooked during the previous harvest?) The small print on the label also brought the disconcerting news that my potato plants were themselves registered as a pesticide with the Environmental Protection Administration (U.S. EPA Reg. No. 524-474).

If proof were needed that the food chain that begins with seeds and ends on our dinner plates is in the midst of revolutionary change, the small print that accompanied my NewLeafs will do. That food chain has been unrivaled for its productivity: on average, an American farmer today grows enough food each year to feed a hundred people. Yet that achievement—that power over nature—has come at a price. The modern industrial farmer cannot grow that much food without large quantities of chemical fertilizers, pesticides, machinery, and fuel. This expensive set of "inputs," as they're called, saddles the farmer with debt, jeopardizes his health, erodes his soil and ruins its fertility, pollutes the groundwater, and compromises the safety of the food we eat. Thus the gain in the farmer's power has been trailed by a host of new vulnerabilities.

All this I'd heard before, of course, but always from environmentalists or organic farmers. What is new is to hear the same critique from industrial farmers, government officials, and the agribusiness companies that sold farmers on all those expensive inputs in the first place. Taking a page from Wendell Berry, of all people, Monsanto declared in a recent annual report that "current agricultural technology is unsustainable."

What is to rescue the American food chain is a new kind of plant. Genetic engineering promises to replace expensive and toxic chemicals with expensive but apparently benign genetic information: crops that, like my NewLeafs, can protect themselves from insects and diseases without the help of pesticides. In the case of the NewLeaf, a gene borrowed from one strain of a common bacterium found in the soil—*Bacillus thuringiensis*, or "Bt" for short—gives the potato plant's cells the information they need to manufacture a toxin lethal to the Colorado potato beetle. This gene is now Monsanto's intellectual property. With genetic engineering, agriculture has entered the information age, and Monsanto's aim, it would appear, is to become its Microsoft, supplying the proprietary "operating systems"—the metaphor is theirs—to run this new generation of plants.

The metaphors we use to describe the natural world strongly influence the way we approach it, the style and extent of our attempts at control. It makes all the difference in (and to) the world if one conceives of a farm as a factory or a forest as a farm. Now we're about to find out what happens when people begin approaching the genes of our food plants as software . . .

St. Louis, June 23. While my NewLeafs were bushing up nicely during a spell of hot early-summer weather; I traveled to Monsanto's headquarters in St. Louis, where the ancient, noble dream of control of nature is in full and extravagant flower. If the place to go to understand the relationship of people and potato was a mountainside farm in South America in 1532 or a lazy bed near Dublin in 1845, today it is just as surely a research greenhouse on a corporate campus outside St. Louis.

My NewLeafs are clones of clones of plants that were first engineered more than a decade ago in a long, low-slung brick building on the bank of the Missouri that would look like any other corporate complex if not for its stunning roofline. What appear from a distance to be shimmering crenellations of glass turn out to be the twenty-six greenhouses that crown the building in a dramatic sequence of triangular peaks. The first generation of genetically altered plants—of which the NewLeaf potato is one—has been grown under this roof, in these greenhouses, since 1984; especially in the early days of biotechnology, no one knew for sure if it was safe to grow these plants outdoors, in nature. Today this research and development facility is one of a small handful of such places—Monsanto has only two or three competitors in the world—where the world's crop plants are being redesigned.

Dave Starck, one of Monsanto's senior potato people, escorted me through the clean rooms where potatoes are genetically engineered. He explained that there are two ways of splicing foreign genes into a plant: by infecting it with agrobacterium, a pathogen whose modus operandi is to break into a plant cell's nucleus and replace its DNA with some of its own, or by shooting it with a gene gun. For reasons not yet understood, the agrobacterium method seems to work best on broadleaf species such as the potato, the gene gun better on grasses, such as corn and wheat.

The gene gun is a strangely high-low piece of technology, but the main thing you need to know about it is that the gun here is not a metaphor: a .22 shell is used to fire stainless-steel projectiles dipped in a DNA solution at a stem or leaf of the target plant. If all goes well, some of the DNA will pierce the wall of some of the cells' nuclei and elbow its way into the double helix: a bully breaking into a line dance. If the new DNA happens to land in the right place—and no one yet knows what, or where, that place is—the plant grown from that cell will express the new gene. *That's it?* That's it.

Apart from its slightly more debonair means of entry the agrobacterium works in much the same way. In the clean rooms, where the air pressure is kept artificially high to prevent errant microbes from wandering in, technicians sit at lab benches before petri dishes in which fingernail-sized sections of potato stem have been placed in a clear nutrient jelly. Into this medium they squirt a solution of agrobacteria, which have already had their genes swapped with the ones Monsanto wants to insert (specific enzymes can be used to cut and paste precise sequences of DNA). In addition to the Bt gene being spliced, a "marker" gene is also included—typically this is a gene conferring resistance to a specific antibiotic. This way, the technicians can later flood the dish with the antibiotic to see which cells have taken up the new DNA; any that haven't simply die. The marker gene can also serve as a kind of DNA fingerprint, allowing Monsanto to identify its plants and their descendants long after they've left the lab. By performing a simple test on any potato leaf in my garden, a Monsanto agent can prove whether or not the plant is the company's intellectual property. I realized that, whatever else it is, genetic engineering is also a powerful technique for transforming plants into private property, by giving every one of them what amounts to its own Universal Product Code.

After several hours the surviving slips of potato stem begin to put down roots; a few days later, these plantlets are moved upstairs to the potato greenhouse on the roof. Here I met Glenda Debrecht, a cheerful staff horticulturist, who invited me to don latex gloves and help her transplant pinkie-sized plantlets from their petri dishes to small pots filled with customized soil. After the abstractions of the laboratory, I felt back on quasi-familiar ground, in a greenhouse handling actual plants.

The whole operation, from petri dish to transplant to greenhouse, is performed thousands of times, Glenda explained as we worked across a wheeled potting bench from each other, largely because there is so much uncertainty about the outcome, even after the DNA is accepted. If the new DNA winds up in the wrong place in the genome, for example, the new gene won't be expressed, or it will be expressed only poorly. In nature—that is, in sexual reproduction—genes move not one by one but in the company of associated genes that regulate their expression, turning them on and off. The transfer of genetic material is also much more orderly in sex, the process somehow ensuring that every gene ends up in its proper neighborhood and doesn't trip over other genes in the process, inadvertently affecting their function. "Genetic instability" is the catchall term used to describe the various unexpected effects that misplaced or unregulated foreign genes can have on their new environment. These can range from the subtle and invisible (a particular protein is over- or underexpressed in the new plant, say) to the manifestly outlandish: Glenda sees a great many freaky potato plants.

Starck told me that the gene transfer "takes" anywhere between 10 percent and 90 percent of the time—an eyebrow-raising statistic. For some unknown reason (genetic instability?), the process produces a great deal of variability, even though it begins with a single, known, cloned strain of potato. "So we grow out thousands of different plants" Glenda explained, "and then look for the best." The result is often a potato that is superior in ways the presence of the new gene can't explain. This would certainly explain the vigor of my NewLeafs . . .

In March 1998, patent number 5,723,765, describing a novel method for the "control of plant gene expression," was granted jointly to the U.S. Department of Agriculture and a cottonseed company called Delta & Pine Land. The bland language of the patent obscures a radical new genetic technology: introduced into any plant, the gene in question causes the seeds that plant makes to become sterile—to no longer do what seeds have always done. With the "Terminator," as the new technique quickly became known, genetic engineers have discovered how to stop on command the most elemental of nature's processes, the plant-seed-plant-seed cycle by which plants reproduce and evolve. The ancient logic of the seed—to freely make more of itself ad infinitum, to serve as both food and the means of making more food in the future—has yielded to the modern logic of capitalism. Now viable seeds will come not from plants but from corporations.

The dream of controlling the seed, and through the seed the farmer, is older than genetic engineering. It goes back at least to the development, in a handful of crops, of modern hybrids, high-yielding varieties that don't "come true" from replanted seed, thereby forcing farmers to buy new seeds every spring. Yet compared to the rest of the economy, farming has largely resisted the trend toward centralization and corporate control. Even today, when only a handful of big companies are left standing in most American industries, there are still some two million farmers. What has stood in the way of concentration is nature: her complexity, diversity, and sheer intractability in the face of our most heroic efforts at control. Perhaps most intractable of all has been agriculture's means of production, which of course is nature's own: the seed.

It's only in the last few decades, with the introduction of modern hybrids, that farmers began to buy their seeds from big companies. Even today a great many farmers save some seed every fall to replant in the spring. "Brown bagging," as this practice is sometimes called, allows farmers to select strains particularly well adapted to local conditions.* Since these seeds are typically traded among farmers, the practice steadily advances the state of the genetic art. Indeed, over the centuries it has given us most of our major crop plants.

Infinitely reproducible, seeds by their very nature don't lend themselves to commodification, which is why the genetics of most of our major crop plants have traditionally been regarded as a common heritage rather than as "intellectual property." In the case of the potato, the genetics of the important varieties—the Russet Burbanks and Atlantic Superiors, the Kennebecs and Red Norlings—have always been in the public domain. Before Monsanto got involved, there had never been a national corporation in the potato seed business. There simply wasn't enough money in it.

Genetic engineering changes this. By adding a new gene or two to a Russet or Superior, Monsanto can now patent the improved variety. Legally it's been possible to patent a plant for several years now, but biologically, these patents have been almost impossible to enforce. Genetic engineering has gone a long way toward solving this problem, since it allows Monsanto to test the potato plants growing on a farm to prove they're the company's intellectual property. The contracts farmers must sign to buy Monsanto seeds grant the company

---

* Worldwide, it's estimated that some 1.4 billion people depend on saved seed.

the right to perform such tests at will, even in future years. To catch farmers violating its patent rights, Monsanto has reportedly paid informants and hired Pinkertons to track down gene thieves; it has already sued hundreds of farmers for patent infringement. With a technology such as the Terminator, the company will no longer have to go to all that trouble.

With the Terminator, seed companies can enforce their patents biologically and indefinitely. Once these genes are widely introduced, control over the genetics of our crop plants and the trajectory of their evolution will complete its move from the farmer's field to the seed company to which the world's farmers will have no choice but to return year after year. The Terminator allows companies like Monsanto to enclose one of the last great commons in nature: the genetics of the crop plants that civilization has developed over the past ten thousand years.

CHAPTER FOUR

POWER, AUTHORITY, AND GOVERNANCE: FOOD AND LAW

In the United States, the regulation of GM foods has been heavily debated, with agribusinesses on one side and consumer awareness groups on the other. For the most part, these two sides rarely agree.

Although biotechnology companies, such as Monsanto, usually work hard to push for less regulation, labeling genetically modified consumer products could potentially work to their advantage. This is due to several factors, including the marketing of GM materials as super foods that provide defense against illness and are packed with every desirable vitamin and mineral.

At the 2001 National Agricultural Biotechnology Conference, Michael F. Jacobson, executive director of the Center for Science in the Public Interest, presented the issues at stake in the labeling debate. He takes an open-minded approach, looking at GM foods from the perspective of the consumer, the farmer, and the food industry. In the end, he makes a number of recommendations on the future uses of biotechnology in agriculture. The following piece is a transcription of his presentation. —SG

From "Agricultural Biotechnology: Savior or Scourge?"
by Michael F. Jacobson
Center for Science in the Public Interest Web Site
May 22, 2001

Biotechnology is reaching a crossroads, where public opposition may become so great that no farmer, food manufacturer, or retailer will want to market a food with biotech ingredients. The biotech industry, by and large, has insisted that genetically engineered foods are sufficiently regulated and perfectly safe. That posture simply isn't flying in the age of StarLink corn, Mad Cow Disease, and the Internet.

Critics are asking many questions about biotechnology —ranging from accusations of potential ecological catastrophes to monopolization of the seed industry by a few companies. The current crops are benefiting primarily the seed and chemical companies and farmers, not consumers. When benefits are enjoyed by one party, but possible risks are borne by another, that's a formula for suspicion. In such an environment, it behooves supporters of biotechnology to address valid concerns, debunk red herrings, and build long-term public confidence by establishing strict rules to protect the environment and ensure safety and choice to consumers.

Before I address the concerns, though, let me emphasize that everyone—including environmentalists—should draw satisfaction from the fact that the current engineered crops appear to have been safe and have yielded environmental benefits.

• According to the National Center for Food and Agriculture Policy, in 1999 Bt cotton enabled farmers to cut their insecticide use by 2.7 million pounds and increase their net revenues by about $100 million. That's a tremendous boon to farmers and presumably to non-target species.

- In 1999, herbicide-tolerant soybeans reduced weed-control costs by $216 million and led to 19 million fewer herbicide applications. The no-till farming that herbicide-tolerant crops encourage also should reduce soil erosion. While overall herbicide usage has remained about the same, glyphosate herbicides appear to be much safer than some of the herbicides that they replaced.
- Bt corn, according to the National Center for Food and Agriculture Policy, saved an estimated 66 million bushels of corn from the European corn borer in 1999. Also, Bt corn should have lower levels of insect damage and some mycotoxins.
- Finally, genetically engineered papayas provide Hawaiian farmers an effective new means of coping with the devastating papaya ringspot virus.

Genetically engineered versions of sweet corn, potatoes, sugar beets, apples, and other crops have been developed and could be providing similar benefits, but farmers and processors won't plant them for fear of a consumer backlash.

Safety Concerns

From the *consumer's* point of view, the key question about biotech foods is, "Are they safe?" To date, of course, biotech foods have not caused any known health problems whatsoever. That record of safety is reassuring. To be honest, though, it probably would be impossible to identify many long-term problems, such as carcinogenicity or neurotoxicity, with current testing procedures.

One of the obvious concerns is whether engineered foods might cause allergic reactions. Known allergens are easy to test for. However, if a protein to which people have had only limited exposure were introduced into foods, one could not state definitively whether that protein could cause allergic reactions.

Another concern is that levels of naturally occurring toxins in plants might be increased. Again, known toxins are easy to test for. But it is not inconceivable that a genetically engineered food would display a novel toxicity, such as by activating a "silent" gene or altering normal metabolic pathways. While speculative, those concerns indicate the need for a rigorous, but not suffocating, regulatory scheme, including appropriate testing standards.

Ecological Concerns

While *consumers* may focus on *safety*, environmental problems may be likelier. Whether it's the effect of Bt corn on non-target organisms, or the spread of genetically engineered characteristics to wild relatives, or the development of pesticide resistance in insects or weeds, GM crops deserve the closest scrutiny. After all, the self-propagating nature of living organisms—be they fish or wheat—means that once a problem occurs, it might be uncontrollable. While the U.S. Department of Agriculture and the Environmental Protection Agency claim to be doing an effective job of anticipating and preventing environmental problems caused by GM crops, last year a committee of the National Academy of Sciences identified numerous ways in which the system should be strengthened. And last March an EPA Science Advisory Panel concluded that data requirements for the effects of Bt corn on non-target insects were not complete, leading the EPA to ask companies for new studies.

Regulation—Safety

Most Americans, I believe, are open to biotechnology, but want assurances that the foods are safe and that crops won't adversely affect the environment. We need to upgrade our regulatory system to minimize those concerns.

The FDA has long relied upon a voluntary consultation process to address any safety problems. That process did not result in any health concerns, but it takes place behind closed doors and does not result in a formal approval. In contrast, the FDA has a mandatory, albeit secret, process for approving transgenic animals—such as fish—and the EPA has a mandatory, relatively open process for evaluating transgenic pest-protected plants, such as Bt corn.

The FDA recently proposed a mandatory review process to replace its current voluntary system for evaluating GM crops. Importantly, the new process would ensure that all new food crops were scrutinized. Also, the new process would be open to public scrutiny, with most company documents being placed on the public record. However, the review process still does not result in a formal approval. Instead, the FDA would say "we have no further questions." While that approach might not result in any harmful mistakes, it would still invite the accurate criticism that transgenic crops are not formally approved in the United States.

Because the FDA has not been willing to formally approve all biotech foods, Congress should mandate that it does so. New legislation should distinguish transgenic organisms from existing categories, such as Generally Recognized As Safe substances or food additives, and establish a formal approval process. Such a new law should ban common or severe allergens from biotech foods, phase out antibiotic-resistance marker genes, and have the National Academy of Science's Institute of Medicine evaluate FDA's standards for biotech foods.

The StarLink episode revealed an additional problem. Farmers and seed producers apparently can't ensure that corn—or other crops—grown for feed will not end up in food. Hence, the FDA and EPA should be prohibited from approving biotech crops for animal feed if they are not also approved for human food.

Those all are simple, sensible measures that the biotech and food-manufacturing industries should be able to accept. Passage of a law that included such measures would significantly enhance public confidence in bioengineered foods.

Regulation—Labeling

The second component of an improved regulatory scheme concerns the labeling of genetically engineered foods. Labeling could respond to concerns ranging from allergies to ethics to environment.

In response to environmental groups, the European Union, Australia, and several other countries are requiring labeling of foods containing engineered ingredients. The FDA has not done so. Instead, the FDA recently announced a *voluntary* labeling scheme that it believes will be useful to consumers. It has described situations in which terms like "does not contain genetically engineered ingredients" may be used on labels. Consumers concerned about GM foods could then choose non-GM products. The FDA's labeling guidance represents a very small advance, and even the FDA admits that very few foods, other than those grown organically, will sprout labels.

Some critics hope that GM labeling would be the kiss of death for engineered foods and agricultural biotechnology. But it may be that the public is simply not going to have confidence in biotechnology if companies are not more open about their use of transgenic ingredients.

To better understand the public's interest in biotech labeling and how consumers might react to such labeling, CSPI recently commissioned a national telephone survey. I'd like to describe some of our findings.

First, 62% to 70% of people said they would like engineered foods to be labeled. Those percentages are similar to many previous surveys and indicate fairly broad support for biotech labeling.

We wanted to get beyond that first question and understand consumer attitudes in greater detail.

The survey found that as the amount of the engineered ingredients in a food decreased, so did the desire for labeling. If labeling were required, 61% of those surveyed said that a whole food, such as a tomato, should be labeled. If a major ingredient, such as the wheat in Wheaties, was engineered, 53% said that that should be labeled. The percentage favoring labeling dropped to 42% for a minor ingredient, such as corn starch in a frozen dinner and to 38% for a food like soy oil that does not contain any engineered material. Thus, if labeling were required, well under half of people wanted labeling when only small amounts of, or no, genetically modified material was present.

We found that people indicate a desire not just for biotech labeling, but for just about any information about food production. Thus, 76% wanted labels to disclose the spraying of pesticides, and 66% wanted information on genetic engineering. But 43% wanted label statements on foods grown with practices that cause soil erosion, and 40% wanted the use of hybrid corn to be disclosed. It could be that most Americans don't know much about food production and are suspicious of any process or term they don't understand. One could interpret such findings as indicating that 40%, not 0%, should be considered the baseline when asking people if they want something on labels about growing practices.

Several questions indicate that support for labeling is not as deep as appears at first glance. We asked people how much extra they would pay for their family's food to have labels declare that foods were genetically engineered. About 60% of the people said they would pay either nothing or only $10 per year for that labeling. One in four respondents said they would pay $50 per year or more for labeling, and a small group of consumers, 12%, said they would pay $250 a year or more to get labeling. Those are the hard-core proponents of labeling. Interestingly, even among those people who said that labeling should be required, half said they would pay nothing or only $10 per year. Thus, although most consumers may desire labeling of GE foods, relatively few appear willing to pay additional costs for that information. Of course, some people might want labeling, but want someone else—namely the food and seed industries—to bear the costs.

We next explored how people interpreted label statements. We found that about one-third of respondents believed that foods labeled "contains genetically engineered ingredients" were not as safe as, or not as good as, foods without labels.

Conversely, about one-third of respondents believed that foods labeled "does *not* contain genetically engineered ingredients" were better than foods without such a label. Thus, if, as appears to be the case, there is no difference in safety or quality between conventional and GM crops, many consumers apparently would be deceived by labels that stated "genetically engineered" or "not genetically engineered."

Those perceptions about safety, quality, or other matters carried over into questions about buying behavior. Only about 40% of respondents said they would buy foods made with genetically engineered ingredients. It didn't matter whether the foods were transgenic fruits and vegetables or processed foods that contained only minor ingredients that came from engineered crops. Clearly, considering the public's current views, no food manufacturer would market foods containing engineered ingredients if they had to put a statement on the label.

We also asked people if they would buy foods bearing other labels. Interestingly, while only 43% of the respondents said they would buy foods labeled "genetically engineered," only about the same percentage said that they would buy foods labeled as having been sprayed with pesticides, treated with plant hormones, or made from cross-bred corn. Apparently, people have apprehensions about *any* unusual and suspicious-sounding statements made on labels.

We did not explore consumers' reactions to different kinds of labels. We left to the imagination of the respondents the prominence of the GM label on food packages. It would be worth exploring how differently people might perceive the term "contains genetically ingredients" on the front of the package, the term "genetically engineered" embedded within the ingredient statement, and a little "GM" symbol somewhere on the front of the package.

If foods are labeled to indicate that they contain, or don't contain, engineered ingredients, the FDA should ensure that labeling does not lead consumers to think that an engineered food is inferior, and that a food made *without* genetically engineered ingredients is superior.

Considering how negatively the public views genetically engineered foods, I think industry needs to play catch-up and be candid with consumers about the benefits and pitfalls of the technology. The seed industry's current expensive ad campaign probably is too vague to have much impact on public thinking. The food industry might be in a position to do a better job. It could mount an advertising campaign depicting hundreds of familiar packaged and restaurant foods that contain ingredients from engineered crops. Those ads could explain the apparent safety and the environmental benefits, while acknowledging that the safety of any food—engineered or not—can never be assured with absolute certainty.

Regulation—Environment

Let me now turn to environmental issues. One major concern is that while the EPA stipulates that certain crops, such as Bt corn, be accompanied by refuges of conventional crops, no agency polices and enforces such important requirements.

That must be corrected. Also, the NAS [National Academy of Sciences] report on pest-protected plants made numerous specific recommendations, ranging from regulating viral coat proteins under FIFRA [Federal Insecticide, Fungicide, and Rodenticide Act] to improving inter-agency coordination. All of those recommendations should be implemented.

Over at USDA, despite the millions of acres planted with GM crops, APHIS [Animal and Plant Health Inspection Service] has never prepared a full Environmental Impact Statement for any of the crops that it approved. Full EISs would have led to better analysis and mitigation for any remaining questions.

To summarize, now is the time, while agricultural biotechnology is still young, for Congress and the regulatory agencies to create the framework that will maximize the safe use of these products.

Other Concerns About Agricultural Biotechnology

Aside from effects on the public's health and the ecosystem, agricultural biotechnology raises many other concerns.

Underlying much of the attacks on biotechnology is the critical question of whether a handful of giant companies—and universities—will end up controlling the world's major crops and the technology itself. The briar patch of patent rights that affected Golden Rice exemplifies the problem. Also, for obvious reason, companies focus on the largest crops in the developed world—and then only on applications that are profitable, rather than ones whose primary purpose is to protect the environment or benefit consumers.

To bring the greatest benefits to the most people, it is essential that government sponsor more basic and applied research to ensure that new methods and products are in the public domain. Government-sponsored research also should address the needs of small farmers, the consumers, and the environment, as well as so-called minor crops. We need creative ways to prevent a thicket of patents from strangling innovation, especially in developing nations. And we need to expand aid programs to train scientists in developing countries, fund research stations, and help those nations build a regulatory structure to anticipate and prevent possible problems.

Organic farmers in the United States have justifiable fears that pollen from biotech farms will pollute their crops, possibly rendering them non-organic, under the law. Organic farmers also fear that insects will develop resistance to Bt toxin. While that concern was always present due to organic farmers' own use of Bt sprays, the widespread planting of Bt corn and cotton increases tremendously the possibility that pests will develop resistance. I don't pretend to have the solutions to those thorny problems, but they deserve careful attention. Buffer zones, compensation by seed companies, and other measures should be developed to protect the integrity of organic foods.

Beyond Biotechnology

Let me conclude by noting that many critics of biotechnology are opposed to any and all applications of biotechnology, apparently regardless of its benefits. Advocates of biotechnology should not fall into a similar trap of thinking that biotechnology is the answer, regardless of the question. Genetic engineering is not the only tool in the agricultural tool box. Conventional breeding and non-transgenic applications of biotechnology offer tremendous opportunity. We should also note that production agriculture, biotech or not, suffers from real problems. Many farmers are going broke—and more would, were it not for huge government bailouts. Both advocates and critics of genetic engineering should recognize that the wisest course of action would be simultaneously to follow *several* paths to satisfy our food needs, making use of genetic engineering, conventional farming, and sustainable approaches. Many farmers are discovering that sustainable agriculture, including organic farming—based on smaller farms, diverse crops, crop rotation, and natural means of pest control—may be just as, or even more, profitable, especially at a time of soaring energy costs. Their input costs may be lower, while their crops may command premium prices in the marketplace.

No big chemical or seed companies, no government subsidies support sustainable agriculture. Hence, my final recommendation would be for ag [agricultural] schools, state departments of agriculture, and USDA to conduct more research and provide greater technical and financial assistance to farmers who want to get off the agribusiness treadmill.

———■———

In the United States, several government agencies are involved with regulating genetically engineered food. The Food and Drug Administration (FDA), the United States Department of Agriculture (USDA), and the Environmental Protection Agency (EPA) all play different roles in this regulatory framework.

The FDA, which has the overall responsibility of mak-
ing sure food is safe to eat, plays the most critical role in the
regulation of GM foods. Current policy states that the FDA
does not need to evaluate GM foods any differently from non-
GM foods. This policy, which has been in effect since 1992,
has sparked a heated debate. Many concerned citizens and
consumer groups feel that this policy is not restrictive enough,
and that GM foods should be evaluated more thoroughly by
the government.

In the following excerpt from her book, Eating in the
Dark, Kathleen Hart describes the current U.S. regulatory
policies concerning GM foods and the controversy that sur-
rounds them. —*SG*

From *Eating in the Dark: America's Experiment with Genetically Engineered Food*
by Kathleen Hart
2003

Three large federal agencies are entrusted with protecting the
American people and the environment from risks that might
arise from genetically engineered plants, foods, animals, and
microbes. Under a regulatory scheme devised during President Ronald Reagan's administration, the Food and Drug
Administration, the Environmental Protection Agency, and the
Department of Agriculture share the task of overseeing the
biotechnology industry. In theory, that sounds like a lot of fire-
power aimed at genetically modified organisms. A look back at
the genesis of this triumvirate, however, reveals that it was

cobbled together more to reassure the public that someone was watching over industry and university scientists than actually to provide robust oversight.

The FDA has overall responsibility for safeguarding the American food supply. It is charged with making sure that a new gene-altered food is safe and nutritious for humans and livestock to eat, and that it contains no new toxins or allergens. The USDA is supposed to ensure that genetically altered plants do not threaten traditional agriculture by spreading undesirable genes to native plants and weeds surrounding the farmlands. The EPA is responsible for protecting the public, wildlife, and the environment from harmful man-made substances. The agency's jurisdiction extends to genetically engineered foods when a plant or microorganism has been engineered to make a pesticide or other toxic substance.

At the time this regulatory framework was devised in the mid-1980s, genetic engineering was a brand-new technology, just over a decade old. In 1973 Herbert Boyer, a researcher at the University of California in San Francisco, and Stanley Cohen, a geneticist at Stanford University, performed a feat that stunned the scientific world: they transferred a gene from one organism to another, thereby creating an entirely new organism. As Eric Grace describes the experiment in *Biotechnology Unzipped*, they first used an enzyme to cut up large bacterial plasmids that contained a gene for resistance to an antibiotic. Plasmids are simple, circular structures found inside bacteria. Next, they cut up the DNA from an African clawed toad. They then mixed the fragments of toad and bacteria genes together, allowing time for them to recombine. When they added living bacteria cells to the mix, they found that DNA from the toad was taken in and copied in the bacteria.

. . . As scientists began to broach natural barriers between species, moving genes from toads into bacteria, chickens into potatoes, and humans into pigs, some members of the general public became alarmed. Intuitively, many people felt that it was unethical or morally wrong to tamper with the natural order of life in so profound a way. Moreover, regardless of their moral or ethical position on the subject of genetic engineering, common sense alone told laypersons that scientists needed to exercise great caution in their laboratories, lest they inadvertently create synthetic organisms capable of causing catastrophic damage to other living organisms . . .

In 1987 the National Academy of Sciences (NAS) released a report that bolstered the idea that potential risks introduced by genetic engineering are no different in kind from risks introduced by selectively crossing two food plants. The NAS is an august body of scientists that is often called upon to advise the government on complex or controversial science policies. The academy assembled a group of five scientists to review the state of the art of genetic engineering and to decide whether the release of genetically engineered microbes, plants, and animals into the environment could present society with any unknown risks.

"No evidence based on laboratory observations indicates that unique hazards attend the transfer of genes between unrelated organisms. Furthermore, there is no evidence that a gene will convert a benign organism to a hazardous one simply because the gene came from an unrelated species," the scientists stated in an influential, slender report entitled

*Introduction of Recombinant DNA—Engineered Organisms into
the Environment: Key Issues.* "Many thousands of distant
genetic transfers have been carried out with R-DNA techniques, and the organisms with the new genes have the
predicted properties: they behave like the parent organism,
but exhibit the new trait or traits expected to be associated
with the introduced gene or genes." Arthur Kelman of the
University of Wisconsin in Madison chaired the NAS panel,
which also included Wyatt Anderson, University of Georgia in
Athens; Stanley Falkow, Stanford University; Nina Fedoroff,
Carnegie Institution of Washington; and Simon Levin, Cornell
University.

Some of the sweeping generalizations that the 1987
NAS panel made would prove overly simplistic in the coming
decade, as scientists and farmers gained experience with gene-
altered plants. In fact, another group of scientists convened by
the NAS in 1999 to review the underpinnings of U.S. regulation of biotech food plants described many ways in which the
process of genetic engineering could potentially give rise to
harmful effects. "Introduction of transgenes into plants typically involves random integration of DNA into the nuclear
genome," the 1999 NAS panel found. The new, modified plant
"might have unexpected traits" or "unintended consequences."

The later panel's findings, however, came too late to
have any effect on the development of the gene-altered corn,
potatoes, soybeans, canola, and other foods that the federal
government approved in the mid-1990s. The 1987 NAS document had provided the scientific rationale for relaxed federal
oversight that allowed genetically modified food crops to begin
entering the American food supply with the 1996 harvest.

In 1990 the Bush administration issued a document entitled "Four Principles of Regulatory Review for Biotechnology" that fleshed out the Reagan administration's 1986 Coordinated Framework with a set of regulatory "principles" aimed at smoothing the way for the speedy development of biotech products. The first principle stated: "Federal government regulatory oversight should focus on the characteristics and risks of the biotechnology product—not the process by which it was created." This federal directive meant that the FDA, the EPA, and the USDA scientists were not supposed to single out genetically engineered foods for review simply because they had been developed using a potent new technology.

This principle struck many critics of genetically engineered food as little more than an empty slogan masquerading as science. It flies in the face of the U.S. patent system, which has ruled that genetically engineered organisms are unique creations for which patent protection can be granted. It is also a position that has isolated the United States from other developed nations: Australia, Austria, Belgium, Denmark, England, France, Germany, Greece, Ireland, Italy, Japan, Korea, the Netherlands, New Zealand, Norway, Portugal, Spain, Sweden, and Switzerland have all elected to treat food plants produced by genetic engineering techniques as different from plants derived through conventional breeding. In those countries, genetically modified food plants are subject to different rules— and to strict labeling requirements—precisely because they are genetically engineered.

Many people find it hard to fathom the logic behind the assumption that the process of genetic engineering poses no unique risks—or that any problems inherent in the process will be revealed by a superficial examination of the end product. Yet the bias against looking for potential problems with the *process* of genetic engineering so thoroughly permeated the U.S. government and scientific establishment that some of the simplest questions about gene-altered foods remain not just unanswered but unasked.

The second of the four principles laid out by the Bush administration called on federal agencies to conduct speedy reviews and to ease the regulatory "burden" on industry. This principle said, "For biotechnology products that require review, regulatory review should be designed to minimize regulatory burden while assuring protection of public health and welfare."

The third principle stated, in part, that any regulatory programs "should be designed to accommodate the rapid advance in biotechnology." This principle enshrined Bush's belief that the expected benefits of biotechnology justified relaxed—if not outright lax—government oversight. The fourth and final principle stated: "In order to create opportunities for the application of innovative new biotechnology products, all regulations in environmental and health areas—whether or not they address biotechnology—should use performance standards rather than specifying rigid controls or specific designs for compliance."

In February 1991, several months after the principles were issued, Vice President Dan Quayle, who chaired the White House Council on Competitiveness, submitted a report to President Bush urging him "to oppose any efforts to create new or modify existing regulatory structures for biotechnology through legislation." Quayle also warned the president, "Foreign nations may seek to ban certain biotechnology products developed in the U.S. without sound scientific basis. They may also attempt to create informal barriers such as labeling and inspection requirements." Quayle's remarks indicated that government and industry leaders fully anticipated a strong negative reaction to genetically engineered foods abroad.

At the end of 1991, several biotech companies were getting ready to take their experimental foods into the marketplace. Calgene was engineering the Flavr Savr tomato. Monsanto was working on Roundup Ready soybeans and a potato engineered to make an insecticide. Calgene and Rhône-Poulenc had an herbicide-resistant cotton plant in the works, and Asgrow Seed Company was testing a virus-resistant squash. Having been bolstered by the four principles, the biotech industry was about to get another lift from President Bush.

On May 29, 1992, the Bush administration announced a new FDA policy on "foods derived from new plant varieties developed via recombinant-DNA technology." The policy stated that genetically engineered foods were to be considered no different from their conventional counterparts unless substantial changes had been made to the nutritional composition of the foods. Companies did not have to label genetically modified foods unless they had inserted a gene from a known allergen, such as a peanut, to the engineered variety or substantially changed its composition. The FDA did not require companies to perform premarket safety tests of genetically altered foods. Nor did they have to notify the FDA of their intention to market new genetically modified whole foods. Instead, companies were encouraged to have a voluntary "consultation" with the FDA. These consultations would take place behind closed doors.

The journal *Bio/Technology* reported that the biotech industry appeared to be "uniformly delighted," even "elated" by the FDA policy. Reporter Jeffrey Fox wrote that in 1992, Richard Godown, president of the Industrial Biotechnology Association in Washington, D.C., told him, "We can bring products to market without unnecessary regulations. But nobody has more incentives to bring safe and natural products to market than the companies." Another biotech industry representative, William Small, executive director of the Washington, D.C.–based Association of Biotechnology Companies, was quoted as saying he was "elated" with the new biotech food policy "because it treats 'food as food, regardless of the process used to produce it.'"

Many consumers who learned about the proposed policy sent the government angry letters. Of the five thousand citizens who submitted comments, 80 percent told the FDA that they wanted the government to require mandatory labels on genetically engineered foods.

. . . Without a requirement that companies issue a premarket notice of their intention to bring out a new biotech food, consumers would have no way of knowing when, or if, a particular food had been genetically engineered. FDA officials, like USDA and EPA bureaucrats, were in close contact with industry executives and knew what kinds of crops genetic engineers were designing. But concerned citizens and independent scientists could not get hold of actual modified foods and test them because none were publicly available. When [FDA Commissioner David] Kessler declared that biotech foods coming from the laboratories of chemical companies were "improved," Americans were forced to take his word on faith.

Unfortunately, the trust that citizens were asked to extend to FDA regulators did not stop there. FDA officials themselves were taking on faith industry's assurances about the safety and benefits of gene-altered foods. The 1992 policy gave industry a free hand to produce whatever genetically engineered foods it wished without pre-market approvals. At the time when the Bush administration developed the FDA policy, there wasn't a single genetically engineered seed on the market for farmers to plant, nor a single biotech vegetable for consumers to buy. Citizens didn't know if these novel food products would first reach the grocery stores in ten months, ten years, or far into the twenty-first century.

. . . FDA scientists had reason to worry that the insertion of foreign genes into a food plant might cause the plant either to produce higher levels of a toxic substance it already makes or to produce a new toxic substance in its edible portion. Naturalists and scientists have long known that food plants contain hundreds of uncharacterized substances, most of which imbue foods with their unique taste, smell, and texture. More than eight hundred "phenolic" substances, which contribute to the bitter taste and sometimes the color of foods, have been detected in plants. Phenolic substances include the tannins found in tea, coffee, cocoa, and grapes, as well as the flavones that give grapefruits and oranges their yellow color.

Many of the plant foods we commonly eat produce dangerous levels of toxins. Over centuries of trial and error, humans have learned to destroy harmful toxins by cooking them, or to avoid eating the poisonous part of a plant. Potato tubers, for example, contain toxins called solanines that, at high levels, can make people sick. Plant breeders in the

United States and many other countries are required to test new varieties of potatoes to make sure the levels of solanines are not too high. Cyanide, found in peach pits and Asiatic varieties of lima beans, can kill people if eaten in high enough doses. A substance called myristicin, which is found in celery, nutmeg, parsley, dill, and black pepper, is also toxic at high levels.

Janet Andersen, who directs the Biopesticides Division of the EPA (which oversees biotech food plants), provided a compelling argument in support of the need for government regulation of new genetically engineered plants. In potato plants, the tubers, if properly cooked, provide a significant source of nutrition for a large part of humanity. But the leaves of the potato plant have natural pesticidal properties and contain a compound that can cause birth defects. If a genetic engineer were to move genes from the potato plant into spinach, in hopes of protecting the spinach plant against insects, the compound that causes birth defects might also be transferred to the spinach leaves, Andersen said during a congressional hearing. The nutritional composition of the genetically modified spinach leaves might remain substantially the same as normal spinach, yet the new plant would certainly raise a possible health risk to consumers.

. . . James Maryanski [the FDA's biotechnology food coordinator] has stated that ultimately it is the company developing a genetically engineered food, not the FDA, that is responsible for the food's safety. "Foods are not required to undergo pre-market approval by FDA. So new varieties of corn, for example, or soybeans, do not necessarily, do not come to FDA for approval before they go to market," he said at a public meeting. The Food, Drug and Cosmetic Act "places the legal responsibility for the safety of these products on the developer, on the purveyor of the product."

The FDA may believe that it is the job of biotech companies to make sure their own foods are safe. But a Monsanto spokesman told a writer for *The New York Times Magazine* that it is up to the FDA to ensure the safety of genetically engineered foods. "Monsanto should not have to vouchsafe the safety of biotech food," Monsanto's director of corporate communications told Michael Pollan, whose insightful article on genetically engineered potatoes was published in the October 25, 1998, issue. "Our interest is in selling as much of it as possible. Assuring its safety is the FDA's job."

FDA officials have argued that U.S. citizens can trust the biotech industry to thoroughly test the safety of genetically engineered foods in-house. Big brand-name companies have too much to lose by marketing dangerous products, agency thinking goes, to allow an unsafe food product on the market. But many consumers and activists in the United States and much of the rest of the world have found little reassurance in this line of reasoning.

When I had a chance to interview Maryanski, he told me the FDA was "very comfortable with the foods that are on the market." I asked him what he thought about the idea put forth by some scientists that genetically engineered foods might have the potential to cause immune system damage or other health problems to humans.

"People can postulate lots of things," Maryanski answered, "and it's not very helpful unless you have some information that you can actually look at to evaluate what's being said. You know, I think that we have looked at all of the genetic material that's been introduced into a plant from the perspective of what is the likelihood that this substance is likely to produce some adverse effect. Now, we can't guarantee the safety of any product that we regulate, whether it's a drug or a food or a food additive. The only thing we can do is make the best judgment based on the information that we have."

———■———

StarLink is a genetically engineered variety of corn used to feed livestock. In September 2000, it was discovered that this strain of corn had made its way onto supermarket shelves. The discovery raised concerns about the Food and Drug Administration's regulation of GM crops and food.

StarLink corn contains Cry9C, an insecticidal protein developed by Aventis CropScience in the 1990s. According to StarLink's online information center, "[The] Cry9C proteins kill insects . . . by destroying the insect's stomach cells . . . StarLink corn seed was registered and annually renewed for domestic animal feed and non-food industrial use in the USA in 1998, 1999 and 2000. The U.S. registration was voluntarily withdrawn by Aventis CropScience in mid-October, 2000."

In the following excerpt from his book, Dinner at the New Gene Café, *Bill Lambrecht takes a look at the controversy surrounding the Cry9C episode, including an examination of the FDA's role in regulating consumer contact with genetically modified foods. —SG*

From *Dinner at the New Gene Café: How Genetic Engineering Is Changing What We Eat, How We Live, and the Global Politics of Food*
by Bill Lambrecht
2001

Cry9C sounds like an exotic chemical or perhaps a gas wafting from a shiny vat in a futuristic novel about frozen people awaiting immortality. In fact, Cry9C is just a tiny protein buried in the dirt. But it's a protein that won a sliver of immortality in the biotechnology debate by prompting reexamination of the United States government's patchwork regulations for genetically modified food.

Cry9C is one of a family of crystalline proteins, known as endotoxins, that come from *Bacillus thuringiensis*, Bt, a naturally occurring soil organism. Bt is deployed by gardeners and organic growers around the world for its insecticidal capabilities, thereby allowing them to avoid chemicals. Starting in the mid-1990s, genetic engineers harnessed Bt's power by splicing it into corn, potatoes, and cotton. Because the Cry proteins from Bt act the same way as insecticides, they sound dangerous. But the Environmental Protection Agency has welcomed them into the environment. They pose no "unreasonable adverse effects" on wildlife, surrounding plants and organisms in the soil, the Environmental Protection Agency reported in 2000.

Besides Cry9C, there's CrylAb delta-endotoxin, approved by the government for use in field corn, sweet corn, and popcorn, and CrylAc, used in several crops.

There's Cry3A in potato plants. But Cry9C, which is approved solely for use in a corn called StarLink, has a distinction: Because of its unknown effects on humans, the EPA decreed that StarLink corn could be eaten only by animals, and not by humans.

"It is not possible for the agency to determine that there is a lack of allergenic potential from Cry9C based upon the available information," the EPA observed, noting that Cry9C does not break down at high temperatures or in stomach gastric juices, and therefore doesn't easily digest. That restriction did not deter Aventis CropScience, a subsidiary of Aventis S.A., of France, and StarLink's manufacturer. In the 2000 planting season, about three hundred thousand acres of StarLink corn were planted in the United States. Aventis told its distributors, who in turn were to tell farmers, that StarLink was meant to be kept separate from other hybrids and to be planted only with buffers to guard against cross-pollination.

In September 2000, an alliance of environmental and consumer advocates calling itself Genetically Engineered Food Alert made a discovery they announced to the world: Supermarkets were selling taco shells that contained Cry9C. The taco maker was no small operator; the activists identified the brand as Taco Bell Home Originals, a product line of Kraft Foods, which is a subsidiary of Philip Morris. The shells in question were sold in lots of twelve and eighteen and in a third package with sauce and seasoning.

The route of these taco shells to groceries offered a tutorial in modern food production. They were made for Kraft in Mexicali, Mexico, by Sabritas Mexicali, a wholly owned subsidiary of PepsiCo. Sabritas in turn had purchased its corn flour from a company called Azteca Milling, which had processed the flour in its mill in the United States, in Plainview, Texas.

Somewhere in the production chain, the StarLink—grown for animals, as is most corn in America—apparently became mixed with other hybrids categorized as yellow corn No. 2. Picture a row of country grain bins that receive corn from many farmers before shipping it elsewhere; perhaps to foreign lands. Here corn from neighboring farmers who planted different seeds becomes blended. Preserving that system of grain mixing along the production trail is one reason food producers and many farmers themselves are fighting against a global campaign to label modified food. They fear that it will hasten the arrival of a two-track commodity food system, requiring costly segregation and testing to keep conventionally grown grains apart from crops derived from genetic engineering.

Genetically Engineered Food Alert is an alliance of seven advocacy organizations: Center for Food Safety, Friends of the Earth, Institute for Agriculture and Trade Policy, National Environmental Trust, Organic Consumers Association, Pesticide Action Network North America, and the State Public Interest Research Groups. The activists had searched for a way to demonstrate the shortcomings of the government, particularly the Food and Drug Administration, in regulating genetically modified food. They knew from working with farmers that just a fraction of the corn grown in the United States is segregated. They knew, too, about StarLink. So they took a chance.

In his shopping cart at a Safeway store in Silver Spring, Maryland, just outside Washington, Larry Bohlen, of Friends of the Earth, piled taco shells and twenty-three products that contained corn. He then shipped them to Genetic I.D., a laboratory in Fairfield, Iowa, for DNA testing. In August, the results for the taco shells had come back positive for Cry9C. Realizing the potential of a faulty result—and the risk of taking on the American government and the country's biggest food producers—the advocates wanted retesting. The results came back the same.

At a news conference in Washington declaring the Cry9C discovery, Genetically Engineered Food Alert demanded a recall of the taco shells and condemned what they regarded as a permissive, largely voluntary method of regulating modified foods in the United States. "It gives the industry the idea that the government is not taking these risks seriously," said Jane Rissler, of the Union of Concerned Scientists. "This is not an imminent health hazard; this is a potential health hazard that is illegally on market, and a government agency should take steps to end that illegal situation." Neither Rissler, a former EPA official, nor members of the alliance could identify a single taco eater who had taken ill or suffered an allergic reaction. Both Kraft and the FDA, which oversees food safety in the United States, said it would look into the matter.

Genetically Engineered Food Alert had already succeeded on two fronts: By winning press attention across the country they planted seeds of doubt about the safety of the new wave of foods. A *New York Times* headline read: "Altered Corn Entering Human Food." Secondly, in identifying an unauthorized food in our diets, the advocates shined a light into apparent gaps in the U.S. regulatory system.

Good Enough?

On paper, America's biotechnology regulation might seem less than reassuring to a mother weighing what to put on the table. The United States—unlike Europe, Japan, and Australia—does not require labeling of genetically engineered foods. Nor were there mechanisms in the regulatory system to find taco shells or any food that might contain genetic materials whose safety remained unproved. It took a public interest group spending over $7,000 to sponsor tests on ground-corn products.

In the United States there is no testing by the government of genetically altered food. Nor in America, biotech incubator of the world, was there mandatory, premarket safety testing by companies. In the case of food additives, the FDA requires tests for allergenicity and toxicity. But by 2001, five years after modified crops began sprouting widely in the United States, safety tests remained voluntary. This rule is consistent with a government decision years ago: In its regulations, the FDA does not differentiate between food derived from genetic modification and food from conventional means. Thus, it does not require additional testing for potential allergens that coalitions of consumers, scientists, and environmentalists have requested. Nor, adhering to the doctrine of "substantial equivalence," does the government require labels on food packaging advising shoppers that food is modified or contains gene-altered ingredients . . .

Stung

Four days after the Cry9C news conference by Genetically Engineered Food Alert, I received a telephone call passing along a rumor: Kraft Foods planned to issue a recall of the Taco Bell shells. I doubted the veracity of what I was hearing. No food had ever been recalled because it had been genetically engineered.

But it was true. Kraft declared that Friday afternoon that they were recalling some 2.5 million boxes of the taco shells from homes and restaurants. "You should not eat any products containing Taco Bell taco shells," Kraft advised on its web site, adding, "at this point, there appears to be no evidence of adverse health effects." Consumers were told that they could return packages of the tacos for refunds. Also, the Taco Bell restaurant chain, which was owned by PepsiCo, announced that their version of the shells, which are made at the same plant in Mexicali, Mexico, were being tested for contamination.

Kraft said it had no knowledge of how the illegal ingredient made it into its corn. "The specifications for the corn Azteca purchased for the taco shells were confined solely to several varieties of conventional yellow corn, and did not include the StarLink corn," the company said.

The company was clearly embarrassed by the controversy swirling around a product that accounted for about $50 million in yearly sales. Stung both by the costly recall and the publicity it had generated, Kraft called on the government to tighten its rules for genetically engineered food. The company said that the government should stop approving engineered corn unless people—and not just animals—can eat it. Moreover, the food giant recommended a mandatory review of all plant biotech work rather than the voluntary system. And if there's not a fully validated testing procedure for identifying GMOs in foods—and often there isn't—those foods should not be approved for the market, Kraft said.

Strikingly, America's biggest food company was making the same arguments as critics demanding that government do a better job of regulating the technology before it became locked irretrievably in the food chain. Agriculture Secretary Dan Glickman said the incident proved that the federal agency needed to do a better job of segregating gene-spliced grains.

And the FDA? The agency called Kraft's recall "prudent," but rejected the suggestion that it had been slow to act. "This is not a case where we have illnesses or health problems," James Maryanski the FDA's biotechnology food coordinator, told the *New York Times*'s Andy Pollack.

———■———

The following excerpt details the rise of Monsanto, an agricultural biotech company based out of St. Louis, Missouri. In the early 1980s, Monsanto began investing heavily in the future of GM crops. First, it hired a number of the best scientists in the United States and asked them to improve upon existing methods of splicing genes into plants. One of Monsanto's first success stories was the development of Roundup Ready soybeans. These crops have a built-in resistance to an herbicide named Roundup, promising farmers the ability to eliminate harmful weeds more effectively.

The success of products like Roundup Ready soybeans relied on having control over the seed industry. Without this control, Monsanto owned the technology but not the means to distribute it to farmers. Monsanto's solution to this problem was to spend $8 billion to purchase a number of seed companies, becoming the world's second-largest provider of seeds. Since then, Monsanto's control of the seed industry, its aggressive business tactics, and its scientific expertise have made it the dominant force in GM crops and food. —SG

From *Lords of the Harvest: Biotech, Big Money, and the Future of Food*
by Daniel Charles
2001

Right up to the time when he put his family's seed company on the auction block, Ron Holden maintained that he had no interest in selling out. Holden's Foundation Seeds was the partner and the guardian of the nation's small, local corn seed companies, he said. He wasn't going to put their fates in the hands of some multinational company concerned only with the bottom line.

Until the 1960s the nation's mom-and-pop seed companies had relied on breeding programs at agricultural universities, which regularly distributed, free of charge, new corn hybrids. But those publicly funded breeding programs gradually fell behind the efforts of Pioneer and DeKalb and closed down. Ron Holden stepped into the gap. Holden's maintained a small but well-run breeding program that delivered new "inbred" lines that became the parents of hybrid seed sold by family-owned seed distributors all over the country. The smallest companies often relied exclusively on Holden's for their seed stock; larger enterprises such as Golden Harvest or Doebler's or even DeKalb used parental lines from Holden's to supplement their own breeding programs. Only Pioneer refused to use any material from Holden's.

When one added it all up, corn lines from Holden's were the immediate ancestors of 40 percent of all the corn grown in the United States. Biotech companies soon realized that Holden's was a gateway for genes, and on the other side of that gate lay tens of millions of acres of corn. By turns biotech executives made their pilgrimages down Interstate 80 across rolling Iowa farm land to the sleepily prosperous town of Williamsburg, Iowa, to see Ron Holden.

DuPont came offering genes for improved oil content. The executive board of AgrEvo flew in from Germany promoting the gene that made corn plants tolerant to the AgrEvo herbicide Liberty. Monsanto came offering Bt genes (which worked well) and genes for tolerance to Roundup (which did not work well in corn).

Ron Holden signed deals with one and all. Monsanto proved to be the most difficult partner.

Executives in St. Louis didn't like the idea of Ron Holden delivering Monsanto's genes to hundreds of small ragamuffin seed operations across the country. For one thing, Monsanto didn't want to endanger its own reputation by entrusting its genes to companies that might not deliver pure batches of seed to their customers. What's more, Monsanto didn't really see any economic benefit in helping the smallest of these companies survive. In Monsanto's view the seed industry needed some consolidation. Fewer seed companies meant less competition and more of a chance for seed companies to raise their prices.

But Ron Holden dug in his heels. His company's whole reason for existence was to help the small seed companies, he said, and he wasn't willing to let Monsanto pick and choose among them. "We made it a condition of our cooperation that we make their genes available to everybody on equal terms," says one top executive at Holden's. In response, as Ron Holden later put it, Monsanto "flushed" Holden's, canceled their cooperation, and forced corn breeders at Holden's to destroy all the plants that contained Monsanto's genes.

A year or two later Monsanto reconsidered, and the two companies started cooperating again. Monsanto also put out the word they were interested in buying Holden's outright. In 1996 bankers from Goldman, Sachs finally convinced Ron Holden that it really was time to cash in the family legacy.

Remembering Monsanto's previous attempts to drop some of his smallest customers, Ron Holden took several steps to prevent any eventual buyer from changing his company's practices too dramatically. The buyer was required to treat all of Holden's customers equally, at least for several years. All of Holden's agreements to produce such traits as Liberty-tolerant corn or DuPont's high-oil corn were to remain intact.

But while Holden was preparing to sell his company, he got a message from DeKalb's lawyers. DeKalb announced that it was in possession of a newly issued patent that made DeKalb, not the German company AgrEvo, the inventor of

Liberty-tolerant corn. DeKalb demanded that Holden's or its customers pay a royalty of twelve dollars for every bag of LibertyLink corn that they sold.

It was an assault on the partnership between Holden's and the German company AgrEvo. "Nobody is going to convince me that it wasn't at the direction of Monsanto. It clearly was," says one bitter AgrEvo executive. After all, Monsanto was one of DeKalb's major shareholders at this point, and Robb Fraley [a Monsanto executive] sat on DeKalb's board. The AgrEvo executive thinks it went something like this: "Monsanto went to Ron Holden and said: 'Take a license to these DeKalb patents and force your customers to do so as well. If you don't, we might have to litigate against you, Ron Holden; and, Ron, that's not going to be pretty. It might blow the whole thing up.' And of course, Ron just wanted to get his billion dollars and go home."

Ron Holden did agree to DeKalb's terms. LibertyLink corn from Holden's thus became more expensive. This severely restricted sales. First in soybeans, then in corn, AgrEvo's gene for Liberty tolerance had been forced to the sidelines.

As bidders lined up to make their offers, such episodes were fresh in their minds. Each company realized that, if it lost the bidding, it might be locked out of a large part of the North American corn seed market. Each made what it considered a highly generous offer. But none came even close to Monsanto's bid. "It was clear that Monsanto was ready to pay anything," says Roderick Stacey, who now runs a consulting group called Verdant Partners and worked with one of the unsuccessful bidders. "Whatever any company was willing to offer or consider, Monsanto was willing to go considerably above that. They just were not going to take the risk that they were not going to get it."

In January 1997 Monsanto announced an agreement to purchase Holden's and the company that distributed the seed company's products for a cool billion dollars. The annual profits of Holden's had never been made public, but they probably didn't exceed a few million dollars. Overnight, Ron Holden became a very rich man.

The Holden's purchase set off gold rush fever for germ plasm. Events cascaded out of control. The landscape of American agriculture seemed to crack and shift, sliding this way and that in response to tectonic forces of remorseless, overwhelming power.

The share price of the Delta and Pine Land Company of Mississippi, which owned some 70 percent of the American market for cottonseed, soared. The shareholders anticipated a merger. They *demanded* a merger, and they owned the company, after all. Roger Malkin, Delta and Pine Land's chairman, lost control of the company he had acquired with farsighted ease a decade and a half earlier.

In northern Illinois the Roberts family, owners of DeKalb, decided that if ever there was a time to sell off the family heirloom, this was it.

Both companies started entertaining offers in 1997 and early 1998, feeding an acquisitive fever in the world of agricultural biotechnology. Executives from Basel and Frankfurt shuttled to New York and back. So did representatives from DuPont in Wilmington. All were scrambling to find secure footing on terrain that Monsanto seemed intent on overturning.

Financial calculations led to discussions of legal rights and possible antitrust concerns. Seeds, those small packages of life, symbols of resurrection and hope, had completed their transformation into economic matter. Germ plasm was king, even in the sterile haunts of Wall Street.

Both deals saw the light of day on May 11, 1998, and Monsanto had the privilege of announcing them both. Robert Shapiro's company revealed that it would pay $2.3 billion for DeKalb and another $1.8 billion for Delta and Pine Land. Once again, according to some involved in the process, no other bidder even came close to Monsanto's offers.

Three weeks later Shapiro dropped another bombshell. Monsanto had agreed to merge with a much larger company, American Home Products, Inc. Monsanto, he explained to stunned employees in St. Louis, was too small. It needed a bigger partner to carry out its dreams and, in particular, to compete in the global pharmaceutical business. Monsanto would be the junior partner in the new merged company when it came to pharmaceuticals. In agriculture it would be the dominant partner.

Finally in July of 1998 Monsanto bought Plant Breeding International, a leading seed company in Great Britain, for half a billion dollars, and three months later Shapiro announced that he would pay $1.4 billion for the international seed businesses of Cargill, operating in Asia, Africa, Europe, and Central and South America.

The grand, $8-billion buying spree was finished. Monsanto was now the world's second-largest seed company, smaller only than Pioneer. Monsanto's reach and influence over the business, however, were much greater than a simple accounting of its seed sales would indicate. Through Holden's Foundation Seeds, Monsanto supplied germ plasm to almost half of the North American market in corn. It dominated most of the soybean market that it did not own through contracts with seed companies that were anxious to sell Roundup Ready seed. It also had established a foothold in seed markets around the globe from Brazil to Indonesia.

CHAPTER FIVE

GLOBAL CONNECTIONS: WHAT THE WORLD WANTS FOR DINNER

Labeling food that contains genetically engineered ingredients is an issue still being explored and debated in the United States. Currently, the United States' policy is that GM foods do not need to be labeled. This is acceptable for many who do not believe GM foods pose a health risk.

However, this is not the case in European countries, where people tend to be overwhelmingly against GM foods. Labeling non–genetically modified food as such is often a point of pride, and many grocery stores have banned the sale of GM products altogether. Critics charge that such practices are often due to groundless and stubborn resistance to change. They claim that these attitudes result in negative publicity concerning GM technology and needlessly prevent millions of people in poorer countries from getting the food they so desperately need. Those against GM foods counter that GM corporations need to do a better job selling the benefits of their products and offer more proof that they do not damage the environment.

In the following article, New York Times *reporter Lizette Alvarez travels to England to learn more about the reasons behind the European resistance to GM foods.* —SG

"Consumers in Europe Resist Gene-Altered Foods"

by Lizette Alvarez
New York Times, **February 11, 2003**

At the Happy Apple greengrocer in this Elizabethan town in England's West Country, the roasted vegetable pasty is labeled, clearly and proudly, as GM-free. So is the hommity pie and a scattering of other products crammed onto shelves.

In fact, all across Britain and most of the rest of Europe, shoppers would be hard pressed to find any genetically modified, or GM, products on grocery store shelves, and that is precisely how most people want it.

Tinkering with the genetic makeup of crops to make them faster-growing and more resilient, something done routinely in the United States with seldom a pang of consumer concern, is seen here as heretical, or at the very least unhealthy.

In some countries, including France and Austria, there is an unofficial moratorium on the sale of genetically modified foods. Such foods simply cannot be found there.

"It's not the natural order of things, that's all," Heather Baddeley, who was picking up lettuce and avocados at the Happy Apple, said about GM foods. "It's a kind of corruption, not the right thing to do, you know?"

Robert B. Zoellick, the United States trade representative, does not agree. He recently called Europe's stance on genetically modified food "Luddite" and "immoral," saying that Europeans' fears about GM foods had persuaded some famine-ridden countries in Africa to reject genetically altered grains.

Some Europeans believed that Mr. Zoellick was in effect blaming Europe for starvation in Africa.

David Byrne, the European Union's health and consumer protection commissioner, said: "The U.S. government, including Republican leaders in Congress, accuse Europe of using the issue of genetically modified food as a way of keeping out American exports." "What Bob Zoellick said over the last few weeks has been unhelpful, clearly. It was unfair. It was wrong."

The European Union finances nongovernmental organizations, but it is those groups themselves, not the European trading bloc, that have moved in some cases to steer Africans clear of genetically altered grains, Mr. Byrne insisted.

"The E.U.'s position on genetically modified food," he added, "is that it is as safe as conventional food."

That may be the official line at European Union headquarters in Brussels. But public sentiment in much of Europe, successfully stoked by environmental groups, is now so fiercely opposed to genetically altered food that in Austria, for example, politicians have won elections by vowing to keep "Frankenfood" at bay.

Many supermarket chains across France, Britain, Italy and Austria, among others, yanked all genetically modified products from their shelves three years ago and are in no hurry to restock them. Most recently, hundreds of Europe's most respected chefs banded together to form a group called Euro-Toques to battle the biotechnology lobby.

American companies like Monsanto stand to make enormous profits if Europe allows the importing of more genetically modified foods.

A decision by the European Parliament on stricter labeling of genetically modified foods could be made as early as summer, and European officials hope that may make the food more acceptable, by clarifying exactly how it is made. But there is concern in the United States that the labeling will only alarm European consumers more.

The proposed rules would trace genetically altered substances in corn, tomatoes, feed and oils and make it clear to consumers which products contained at least 0.9 percent of a genetically modified substance. The products concerned include highly refined corn oil, soybean oil and glucose syrup produced from cornstarch.

In France and Italy, Europe's two food meccas, public revulsion at GM food runs especially deep.

"U.S. culture is different from European culture," said Lorenzo Consoli, a Greenpeace expert on genetic engineering. "Here, there is a very strong feeling that links culture and food. And here there is much more the idea that science is not church or a religion. It is not enough anymore for European consumers to have somebody with a white coat, a professional, say it's O.K."

A string of food scandals, including the outbreak of mad cow disease in 1996, severely undermined people's faith in the safety of their food and their confidence in scientists and public officials, many of whom asserted that consumers faced no health risk at the time.

Other scandals—H.I.V.-tainted blood in France, the spread of mad cow disease from Britain to other European nations, and dioxin-infested chickens in Belgium—only added to the mistrust.

Although there is no compelling evidence so far that genetically altered food is harmful, anti-GM activists say it is unknown whether the food is harmful in the long term. The uncertainty is precisely what worries Europeans.

Europeans also tend to be more environmentally sensitive than Americans, and environmental groups like Greenpeace and Friends of the Earth carry much greater sway.

One widespread fear is that genetically altered crops will pollinate and infest neighboring crops, affecting ecosystems in unpredictable, and perhaps irreversible, ways. Environmental groups have turned that concern into a successful campaign against genetically modified food.

Europeans also care more than Americans about how food tastes, as opposed to how long it can sit on a shelf. "For some member states it's nearly synonymous with sovereignty," said Mr. Byrne, referring to the quality of food. The fight against genetically modified food is being led by organizations, like Greenpeace, which is rooting for a legal confrontation over the issue in the World Trade Organization.

Pia Ahrenkild Hansen, the spokeswoman for the European Union environmental commissioner, said the industry had done a poor job of marketing the advantages of genetically modified foods in Europe.

"The industry has been incredibly bad about demonstrating what's the benefit," Ms. Hansen said. "Why it would make food production more sustainable. Why it would require less resources. Those arguments are not known by the consumers. People say, 'Why should we buy it?'"

In this speck of a town in the county of Devon, it is almost impossible to find any supporters of genetically modified foods. Three weeks ago, the county council's executive board endorsed a decision to bar its schools and hospitals from using any genetically altered food.

Angry citizens held marches, set up booths and attended meetings on the issue. Residents were especially incensed when Britain began a set of trials of genetically modified foods on farms, one of which is near here.

One district councilor, Anne Ward, is petitioning the South Ham district here to declare itself a "GM-free zone." Ms. Baddeley, and many other shoppers at the Happy Apple, would favor that without a second thought, they said.

———■———

For farmers, one of the key selling points of genetically engineered seeds lies in economics. Monsanto's Roundup Ready soybeans, which entered the commercial market in 1997, were quickly bought up by U.S. and Argentinean farmers eager to find solutions to their economic troubles. In Colonia Loma Senés, a small farming village in Argentina, farmers soon took to planting almost exclusively Monsanto's GM soybeans, which were resistant to an herbicide manufactured, not coincidentally, by Monsanto. The government did little to regulate the use of the Monsanto seeds, and soon herbicide-resistant weeds began to grow up around the crops, which the farmers doused with larger and larger amounts of herbicide. Eventually, local crops and livestock died from massive exposure to these chemicals.

In the following article, Sue Branford, a journalist who specializes in environmental issues, takes a look at the situation in Argentina to better understand the complications of farming genetically modified crops. —SG

"Argentina's Bitter Harvest"
by Sue Branford
New Scientist, April 17, 2004

A year ago, Colonia Loma Senés was just another rural back-water in the north of Argentina. But that was before the toxic cloud arrived. "The poison got blown onto our plots and into our houses," recalls local farmer Sandoval Filemón. "Straight away our eyes started smarting. The children's bare legs came out in rashes." The following morning the village awoke to a scene of desolation. "Almost all of our crops were badly damaged. I couldn't believe my eyes," says Sandoval's wife, Eugenia. Over the next few days and weeks chickens and pigs died, and sows and nanny goats gave birth to dead or deformed young. Months later banana trees were deformed and stunted and were still not bearing edible fruit.

The villagers quickly pointed the finger at a neighbouring farm whose tenants were growing genetically modified soya, engineered to be resistant to the herbicide glyphosate. A month later, agronomists from the nearby National University of Formosa visited the scene and confirmed the villagers' suspicions. The researchers concluded that the neighbouring farmers, like thousands of others growing GM soya in Argentina, had been forced to take drastic action against resistant weeds and had carelessly drenched the land—and nearby Colonia Loma Senés—with a mixture of powerful herbicides.

The villagers took their neighbours to court and won an order banning further spraying. The judge also found the tenants guilty of "causing considerable harm to crops and human health." But it was a pyrrhic victory. In September, new tenants took over the land and started spraying again. When challenged, the farmers said that the ban did not apply to them, which was technically true.

Colonia Loma Senés is not an isolated case. Over the past eight years, GM soya farmers have taken over a huge proportion of Argentina's arable land, leading to regular complaints by peasant families that their crops have been harmed by glyphosate and other herbicides. "We really don't know how much damage is being done throughout the country, because the authorities are not monitoring the situation properly," says Walter Pengue, an agro-ecologist from the University of Buenos Aires who has studied the impact of GM soya. But he predicts that such incidents will become more common as a consequence of Argentina's rush into GM soya. And other experts are warning of potential problems that include the emergence of herbicide-resistant weeds and destruction of the soil's natural micro-organisms.

GM technology is not entirely to blame for Argentina's agricultural woes. Economic problems have also played their part. But the country's experience with GM soya holds worrying lessons for the rest of the world, particularly developing countries such as Brazil, the world's second largest soya producer after the US. After refusing for years to authorise GM technology, Brazil is now rethinking its policy. Farmers in the south have been illegally planting GM soya smuggled over from Argentina, attracted by reports of higher yields and lower production costs. This has left the government with little option but to accept the cultivation of GM soya as a fait accompli. Last year it reluctantly gave temporary authorisation for the sale of GM soya on the domestic market and is now debating the finer details of permanent approval. Argentina's experience suggests that Brazil would do well to opt for tight controls with rigorous environmental impact studies.

In 1997, Argentina became one of the first countries to authorise GM crops, when Monsanto's Roundup Ready soya was introduced there and in the US. This GM variety is resistant to glyphosate, which Monsanto sells under the trade name Roundup. Argentina's farmers jumped at the new technology, which seemed just what they needed to solve some of their most pressing problems. Since the late 1980s, Argentina's largest and most fertile farming region, the Pampas, had been suffering from serious soil erosion. About half of the 5 million hectares of the Pampas's core grain-producing region was suffering severe erosion, according to the country's National Institute of Agricultural Technology (INTA), and yields on these lands had fallen by at least a third. To try and alleviate the problem, farmers were experimenting with no-tilling—a system in which seed is sown directly on the land without ploughing or any other form of cultivation. But with no ploughing, weeds were starting to get out of control, and the farmers were at a loss as to what to do.

Roundup Ready soya seemed a solution made in heaven. Farmers were able to make the no-till system work because, instead of needing five or six applications of various herbicides, they could spray only twice with glyphosate at key moments in the season. What's more, the seed companies made the move into Roundup Ready easy by supplying the seeds, machinery and pesticides in a single convenient "technological package." The new technology was also cheap. While farmers in the US paid a premium of at least 35 per cent to plant GM varieties, Argentina had not at that time signed an international patent agreement so Monsanto was able to charge only a modest fee or risk being undercut by companies making generic copies of its technology.

Driven by the world's apparently insatiable demand for soya to feed to cattle, Argentinian farmers stampeded into soya, one of the few profitable sectors in a depressed economy. Desperate to join in, urban investors rented land from impoverished smallholders and turned it over to soya. Anta, the farming group that did the damage to Colonia Loma Senés, benefited from such schemes.

By 2002 almost half of Argentina's arable land—11.6 million hectares—was planted with soya, almost all of it GM, compared with just 37,700 hectares of soya in 1971. Soya moved beyond the Pampas into more environmentally fragile areas, especially in the northern provinces of Chaco, Santiago del Estero, Salta and Formosa. Not even Monsanto had imagined that the move into Roundup Ready soya would be so rapid.

At first everything looked rosy. From 1997 to 2002 the area under soya cultivation increased by 75 per cent and yields increased by 173 per cent. In the early years there were also clear environmental benefits. Soil erosion declined, thanks to the no-till method, and farmers moved from more damaging herbicides to glyphosate, widely regarded as one of the least toxic herbicides available.

Even when world soya prices started to decline as global supply increased, Argentinian farmers continued to do well financially. Monsanto progressively cut the price of Roundup and by 2001 it was selling at less than half its 1996 price. Overall, Argentina's farmers made a profit of about $5 billion by adopting Roundup Ready soya.

Some years ago, however, a few agronomists started to sound alarm bells, warning that the wholesale and unmonitored shift into Roundup Ready soya was causing unforeseen problems. In a study published in 2001 by the Northwest Science and Environmental Policy Center, a non-profit organisation in Sandpoint, Idaho, agricultural economics consultant Charles Benbrook reported that Roundup Ready soya growers in Argentina were using more than twice as much herbicide as conventional soya farmers, largely because of unexpected problems with tolerant weeds. He also found that they were applying glyphosate more frequently than their US counterparts—2.3 versus 1.3 applications a year. Saying that "history shows us that excessive reliance on any single strategy of weed or insect management will fail in the long run, in the face of ecological and genetic responses," he advised Argentinian farmers to reduce their Roundup Ready acreage by as much as half in order to cut glyphosate usage. If they did not, he warned, they would run the risk of serious problems. Among his predictions were shifts in the composition of weed species, the emergence of resistant superweeds, and changes in soil microbiology.

The warning fell on deaf ears. Argentina's economy was in deep trouble, and with soya now its main export earner the government was in no mood to intervene. The area under Roundup Ready has continued to grow, and farmers hurt by the collapse of Argentina's currency at the end of 2001 are increasingly moving into soya monoculture, as other crops

for the domestic market have become unprofitable. Glyphosate
use continues to rise. Pengue estimates consumption reached
150 million litres in 2003, up from just 13.9 million litres
in 1997.

Initially Pengue believed that with careful rotation of
crops and adequate controls over the way the herbicide was
applied, the move to glyphosate would benefit the environment. But he is now concerned that the unmonitored use of
this one herbicide is leading to the problems predicted by
Benbrook. In a study into the impact of Roundup Ready
soya on weeds, Delma Faccini of the National University of
Rosario found that several previously uncommon species
of glyphosate-tolerant weed had increased in abundance.
In another study, agronomists from INTA's office in Venado
Tuerto, near Rosario, found that farmers were having to use
higher concentrations of glyphosate. For now, the problem
appears to be limited to the proliferation of weeds that are
naturally resistant, but some agronomists are warning that it
is only a matter of time before glyphosate resistance is transferred to other weed species, turning them into superweeds.

The third problem that was predicted by Benbrook—
changes in soil microbiology—also appears to be happening.
"Because so much herbicide is being used, soil bacteria are
declining and the soil is becoming inert, which is inhibiting the
usual process of decomposition," says agronomist Adolfo Boy
from the Grupo de Reflexión Rural, a group of agronomists
opposed to GM farming. "In some farms the dead vegetation
even has to be brushed off the land." He also believes that
slugs, snails and fungi are moving into the newly available
ecological niche.

Similar problems are occurring to some extent in the US. According to Joe Cummins, a geneticist from the University of Western Ontario in Canada, studies of the impact of herbicides, particularly glyphosate, on soil microbial communities have revealed increasing colonisation of the roots of Roundup Ready soya with the fungus *Fusarium* in Midwestern fields.

Argentina's farmers are also having to deal with the proliferation of "volunteer" soya, which sprouts from seeds dropped during harvest and which cannot be eradicated with normal doses of glyphosate. This has created marketing opportunities for other agrochemical companies such as Syngenta, which has been placing adverts with the slogan "Soya is a weed" advising farmers to use a mixture of paraquat and atrazine to eradicate volunteer soya. Other companies, including Dow AgroSciences, are recommending mixing glyphosate with other herbicides, such as metsulfuron and clopyralid.

Market Forces

Not all scientists in Argentina are convinced that the farmers' problems have been caused by heavy use of glyphosate, and others say that the difficulties are not yet critical. "We are experiencing some problems of tolerant weeds, but they are not on a large enough scale to affect overall yields seriously or to jeopardise the future of soya farming," says Carlos Senigalesi, director of investigative projects at INTA. He believes it is the tendency for farmers to grow nothing but soya, rather than the prevalence of GM strains, which is at the root of the problem. "Monoculture is not good for the soils or for biodiversity and the government should be encouraging farmers to return to crop rotation," Senigalesi says. "But here everything is left to the market. Farmers have no proper guidance from the authorities. There are no subsidies or minimum prices. I think we must be the only country in the world where the authorities do not have a proper plan for agriculture but leave everything to market forces."

For the first time however, INTA recently expressed concern. In a report published in December it criticised "the disorderly process of agricultural development," warning that if nothing was done, a decline in production was inevitable and that the country's "stock of natural resources will suffer a (possibly irreversible) degradation both in quantity and quality." It called for changes in farming practices in the Pampas, saying that the combination of no-till with soya monoculture was "not a sustainable alternative to crop rotation farming." It also warned that, in the north, soya farming "is not compatible with the sustainability of farming."

Monsanto's Argentinian headquarters has refused to comment directly on these accusations. But the company has expressed concern about the situation, saying it believes that crop rotation is more sustainable than monoculture. It is also starting to suffer from the lack of government controls. In January it unexpectedly halted sales of Roundup Ready soya, saying that farmers were buying about half of their seeds on the black market and depriving the company of royalties.

To Benbrook, this adds up to a very worrying outlook. "Argentina faces big agronomic problems that it has neither the resources nor the expertise to solve," he says. "The country has adopted GM technology more rapidly and more radically than any other country in the world. It didn't take proper safeguards to manage resistance and to protect the fertility of its soils. Based on the current use of Roundup Ready, I don't think its agriculture is sustainable for more than another couple of years."

Argentina used to be one of the world's major suppliers of food, particularly wheat and beef. But the "soyarisation" of the economy, as the Argentinians call it, has changed that. About 150,000 small farmers have been driven off the land. Production of many staples, including milk, rice, maize, potatoes and lentils, has fallen sharply.

Many see Argentina's experience as a warning of what can happen when production of a single commodity for the world market takes precedence over concern for food security. When this commodity is produced in a system of near monoculture, with the use of a new and relatively untested technology provided by multinational companies, the vulnerability of the country is compounded. As yet, few countries have opted for GM technology: the US and Argentina together account for 84 per cent of the GM crops planted in the world. But as others, including the UK, seem increasingly prepared to authorise the commercial growing of GM crops, they may be well advised to look to Argentina to see how it can go wrong.

Worldwide opinion concerning GM technology varies widely. In Africa, most countries remain opposed to transgenic crops. Only a few, including South Africa, and most recently Tanzania, allow these crops to be grown on their land. In 2001, the United Nations warned African countries that, until more is known about long-term effects of such crops, they should not be relied on as a way to produce more food and improve national economies.

Europe has traditionally been strongly opposed to GM technology. However, according to the following article from the Economist, *the resistance shows signs of sputtering out, at least in Great Britain. Consumer opinion, though, is always subject to change. If predictions of disaster resulting from the introduction of GM seeds into the environment pan out, the fallout will swiftly affect the public's consumption and support of GM foods across the globe.* —SG

"Far Less Scary Than It Used to Be"
Economist, July 24, 2003

In Rochford, east of London, two dozen people gathered recently to discuss their hopes and fears about genetically modified (GM) food. The assembled housewives, pensioners and farmers listened politely to a handful of guest speakers, and then they fired off questions: How can you be sure that GM food is safe to eat? Aren't GM crops hurting the environment? Will GM feed the world's poor?

Such questions have been asked up and down Britain. The meeting in Rochford was one of more than 450 public gatherings in a month-long consultation exercise called "GM Nation?". The exercise, which ended last week, is only one of several studies commissioned by the British government. Earlier this month, the Cabinet Office, a government department, published an assessment of the costs and gains of Britain embracing, or rejecting, GM agriculture. This week, a group led by the government's chief science adviser published a review of the scientific evidence of the risks and benefits of GM crops. Soon a committee will flesh out the guidelines issued by the European Commission this week on how GM and non-GM (particularly organic) agriculture can co-exist, and who should pay if one contaminates the other. Then in September the results of about 200 field trials looking into the effects of GM crops on the country's bugs and birds will be published.

The last time Britain saw such a flurry of interest in GM food was in 1999, when a series of events turned much of the population against "Frankenfoods" and drove the stuff from supermarket shelves. The upshot was a "voluntary" moratorium on the commercial cultivation of GM crops in Britain, a pause which the government has said it will reconsider in the autumn.

The results are of interest far beyond Britain. The battle over GM foods has pitted the world's main producers—America, Argentina and Canada—against the European Union and others that resist its spread. This may well culminate in a fully-fledged trade war at the World Trade Organisation (WTO) if America presses ahead with its complaint that the EU's five-year de facto moratorium is a scientifically unjustifed trade barrier.

Out in the Field

At issue are two broad types of genetic modification, which account for 99% of the almost 59m hectares of GM crops in commercial cultivation. One, called Bt, takes a gene from a bacterium and puts it in plants to give them resistance to certain insects without the use of chemical pesticides. The other uses genes also from bacteria and gives plants resistance to particular herbicides, such as glyphosate.

The main GM crops—soyabeans, maize, cotton and oilseed rape—are now grown commercially in 16 countries and tested in a dozen more. GM commodities are also widely traded, even in the European Union which still imports several GM products, such as soya meal for animal feed. Spain actually grows some GM crops commercially.

Much of the resistance to GM food stems from concern over its potential risks to human health and the environment. This week's review of the scientific evidence in Britain concludes, as several other expert bodies have before it, that there is no evidence to suggest that today's GM crops are less safe to eat than conventional foods. In many countries, GM foods are already heavily scrutinised for nutritional content, toxicity, allergenicity and genetic stability before being allowed on to the market. While the British review is sanguine about today's GM foods, it also recommends more research and longer-term studies on future generations of the stuff.

The case for eating GM crops is far clearer than for planting them. In the late 1990s, opponents of GM technology predicted ecological catastrophe from introducing these "unnatural" creations into the landscape. One of their fears was that the pests which farmers most want to kill off, such as the European corn borer, would develop resistance to the Bt toxin in GM plants.

However, studies of Bt cotton in America and China have shown that, after seven years of commercial planting, the target pests are still as vulnerable to the toxin as ever. But this is no cause for complacency, says Bruce Tabashnik, an entomologist at the University of Arizona. He believes it is only a matter of time before resistance develops—as it has to every other pesticide ever tried.

Then there are worries about gene flow—the wafting of pollen or seed from a GM plant to an unmodified one, and the passing on of undesirable characteristics. This happens as a matter of course between conventional crops, so it should be no surprise that it happens with GM plants, says Allison Snow, a plant biologist at Ohio State University. The consequences depend on the circumstances. Gene flow from one field of GM maize to another may make little difference in the middle of Nebraska; a similar flow in, say, Mexico, home to thousands of wild relatives of the domesticated maize plant could have serious repercussions.

A further worry is over GM plants' potential to harm everything from microbes in the ground to songbirds overhead. America was in a flap four years ago when experiments suggested that GM maize could poison Monarch butterflies: field tests later suggested that such an event was highly unlikely.

Scientists do not have a clear view of the full ecological impact of GM crops, or indeed of conventional farming, says Angelika Hilbeck, an ecologist at the Swiss Federal Institute of Technology. For every study suggesting that GM crops can boost, say, insect numbers by replacing brutal chemicals with more environmentally friendly products, there is another showing problems for the birds and the bees.

On the whole, according to this week's review of the science in Britain, the GM crops that are now being grown commercially are no worse for the environment than conventional farming. Indeed, under proper management, some of them can be better for it. That said, there are limits to the extent to which the experience of, say, Saskatchewan can be applied to Somerset. Ecosystems and agricultural practices vary greatly around the world, and the review calls for much more research into the local effects of GM.

Sow What?

While biology can go some way to answering uncertainties about GM crops, the future of the technology lies with a more dismal science: economics. Crucial here is the demand for GM products along the food chain, from farm to fork. In America, there is certainly some home-grown resistance to GM food, but consumers are generally unperturbed by having GM crops in their backyard or on their dinner plates.

In Europe, opinion polls suggest that public attitudes towards GM food have mellowed from outright distaste at the end of the 1990s to cautious uncertainty. "The advocates of GM technology are wrong when they say that public resistance is based on a misperception of risk," says George Gaskell, a sociologist at the London School of Economics. "Rather, it stems from an apparent lack of benefit."

Four years ago, several big international companies, Monsanto among them, were promising consumers a brave new world of healthier, better-tasting GM foods. But it has been slow to appear. Today there are consumer-friendly GM crops in the works—tomatoes high in heart-protecting anti-oxidant molecules, for example—but it will be many years before they appear in a market near you.

Moreover, the firms in the business are not as robust as they once were. Monsanto and Syngenta, formerly part of profitable pharmaceutical companies, are now independent operations and no longer have the same deep pockets for GM research or for purchasing seed companies. Syngenta has shifted some of its focus to industrial applications of GM plants, such as producing pharmaceuticals, that might gain easier acceptance in Europe than GM foods.

This tolerance will quickly evaporate, however, if one slips into the human food supply. America has already had a couple of such scares. In one, a variety of GM maize, used for animal feed but not approved for human consumption, made its way into taco shells. Hundreds of millions of dollars-worth of processed food and raw grain had to be destroyed.

This failure to enthuse consumers comes as no surprise to Lawrence Busch, an agribusiness expert at Michigan State University. Historically, firms such as Monsanto and Syngenta, which had their origins in agrochemicals, saw farmers, not shoppers, as their main customers. So when they turned to biotechnology in the 1990s to help boost their flagging sales and offset high development costs, such companies focused on easy traits that would be of immediate interest to farmers, their traditional customer, rather than to food manufacturers or shoppers.

Most farmers who have tried GM crops since they first started to spread commercially in the mid-1990s like them, which is why acreages expanded by more than 10% last year. And this is despite the higher cost of the seed and the strict conditions that companies often attach to their contracts of sale. There is even a thriving market in smuggled seed in Brazil, where the government has not yet formally authorised commercial planting. Up to one-third of Brazil's soyabean acreage is GM, according to Tray Thomas, an agribusiness expert in Des Moines, Iowa.

The specific benefits conferred on farmers vary. In general, though, those who turn to, say, herbicide-resistant soyabeans, do not plant them for higher yields. GM versions are not much more productive than conventional varieties. Rather, farmers choose them because they are easier to manage, demand less weeding and take lower-cost, less toxic herbicides. Bt crops, on the other hand, can produce higher yields than ordinary ones, under certain circumstances. They also need less insecticide, which is better for health and, maybe, for the environment too.

Leonard Gianessi of the National Centre for Food and Agriculture Policy in Washington, DC, reckons that eight different commercially grown GM crops in America, from herbicide-resistant soyabeans in Minnesota to virus-resistant papaya in Hawaii, boosted American farm income by $1.5 billion in 2001. Studies in Argentina, China, South Africa and Spain have also shown that farmers can gain. On the other hand, Britain's Soil Association, an organic farmers' trade association and opponent of GM crops, can point to studies showing that farmers in America, at best, only break even from their use of GM.

The bottom line, says Michigan State University's Mr. Busch, is that farmers generally see cost advantages from GM crops—or they would not keep planting them. But in its recent economic review, Britain's Cabinet Office noted that the financial benefits that might accrue to British farmers from planting, say, herbicide-resistant oilseed rape are unlikely to compensate for the lack of a market should their main customers shun the stuff. Indeed, having GM on the farm could add to costs throughout the food chain. New European rules on labelling and traceability, to come into force later this year, will demand further careful separation of GM and non-GM crops, and a detailed paper trail from field to foodstore.

The rules will also require that the distinction between GM and non-GM be applied to animal feed and "derivatives"— such as soya oil—which appear in a wide variety of processed foods. When consumer-oriented GM foods reach the market, producers may welcome these new regulations as a way of singling out higher-value products. But in the absence of a premium for GM foods, they are seen by the food industry as an onerous extra cost.

What's in It for Me?

The essential problem for GM foods is that farmer-friendly crops do not, at present, translate into comparable benefits further down the food chain. Archer Daniels Midland, one of the world's leading grain handlers, does not see a big difference between the price of GM and of conventional produce. Food manufacturers, such as General Mills, are equally sceptical about the advantage to consumers in GM food. At the same time, the message coming from some of Europe's powerful supermarkets is that they don't want to stock anything that they have to describe as GM.

For all their complaints about foreign opposition to GM crops, however, there is, as yet, little sign that farmers in America or Argentina are abandoning the technology in droves. Those who do, in order to cater to GM-wary markets, expect a premium. Non-GM soya exports to Japan, for example, command a premium of around 10%.

But Europe's resistance to GM foods is having an effect beyond its borders. In Canada, for example, there is a fierce row in the prairies over Monsanto's new GM wheat. The company claims that it will greatly assist farmers in weed control, thereby reducing farm costs. But the Canadian Wheat Board is advising farmers not to plant it, since much of their produce makes its way to export markets in Europe, which might be jeopardised if GM material were to sneak in. Countries from China to Zambia have also seized upon Europe's resistance to GM to justify their own import barriers. On the other hand, new markets are opening elsewhere to cater to GM-wary populations: one country's trade loss is another's golden opportunity.

Far from taking over world agriculture, GM crops represent less than 5% of world farm acreage. Hesitant markets, as well as scientific uncertainty, will continue to slow their spread in Europe and Asia. For all the extravagant promises of salvation, and the dire predictions of damnation, the past five years of public resistance have brought GM technology down to earth. Its future now lies in more focused applications in particular parts of the world. GM never did stand for Global Miracles.

TIMELINE

8,000 BC —— Agriculture begins in the Near East. Earth's population soars to 5.3 million, up from 3 million in 10,000 BC.

1,500 BC —— All major food plants that will be used in the twentieth century, with the exception of the sugar beet, are being cultivated somewhere in the world.

1715 —— Thomas Fairchild creates Europe's first hybrid plant.

1870– 1890 —— Plant researchers crossbreed cotton to develop hundreds of new varieties.

1908 —— First U.S. hybrid corn is produced by G. H. Shull of the Carnegie Institute.

1930 —— U.S. Congress passes the Plant Patent Act, enabling the products of plant breeding to be patented.

1933 —— Hybrid corn becomes available commercially in the United States, causing yields to triple in fifty years.

1953 —— James Watson and Francis Crick describe the double helix structure of DNA, providing valuable insight into how DNA carries genetic information.

1960s —— Norman Borlaug creates dwarf wheat that increases yields by 70 percent, launching the green revolution.

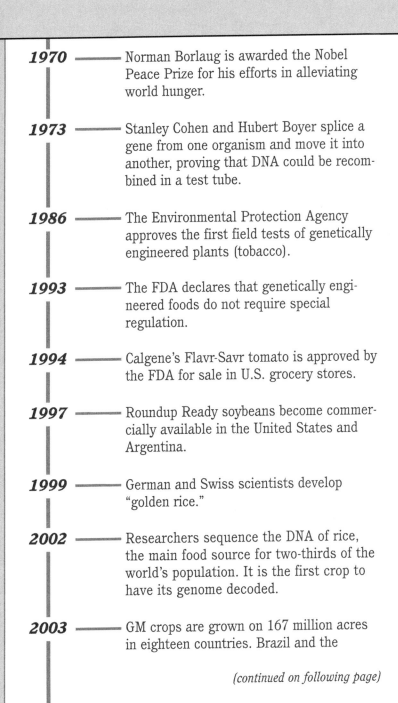

1970 — Norman Borlaug is awarded the Nobel Peace Prize for his efforts in alleviating world hunger.

1973 — Stanley Cohen and Hubert Boyer splice a gene from one organism and move it into another, proving that DNA could be recombined in a test tube.

1986 — The Environmental Protection Agency approves the first field tests of genetically engineered plants (tobacco).

1993 — The FDA declares that genetically engineered foods do not require special regulation.

1994 — Calgene's Flavr-Savr tomato is approved by the FDA for sale in U.S. grocery stores.

1997 — Roundup Ready soybeans become commercially available in the United States and Argentina.

1999 — German and Swiss scientists develop "golden rice."

2002 — Researchers sequence the DNA of rice, the main food source for two-thirds of the world's population. It is the first crop to have its genome decoded.

2003 — GM crops are grown on 167 million acres in eighteen countries. Brazil and the

(continued on following page)

Philippines grow GM crops for the first time. China and Uganda begin accepting GM crop imports.

2004 ——— The United Kingdom approves its first GM crop (corn) for commercial farming.

FOR MORE INFORMATION

Biotechnology Industry Organization
1225 Eye Street NW, Suite 400
Washington, DC 20005
(202) 962-9200
Web site: http://www.bio.org

Council for Responsible Genetics
5 Upland Road, Suite 3
Cambridge, MA 02140
(617) 868-0870
Web site: http://www.gene-watch.org

Food Policy Institute
3 Rutgers Plaza
New Brunswick, NJ 08901
(732) 932-1966
Web site: http://biotech.foodpolicyinstitute.org

Web Sites

Due to the changing nature of Internet links, the Rosen
Publishing Group, Inc., has developed an online list of Web
sites related to the subject of this book. This site is updated
regularly. Please use this link to access the list:

http://www.rosenlinks.com/canf/gmcf

FOR FURTHER READING

Borem, Aluizio, Fabricio R. Santos, and David E. Bowen. *Understanding Biotechnology*. London, England: Franklin Watts, 1999.

Cummins, Ronnie. *Genetically Engineered Food: A Self-Defense Guide for Consumers*. New York, NY: Marlowe & Company, 2000.

Dawkins, Kristin. *Gene Wars: The Politics of Biotechnology*. New York, NY: Seven Stories Press, 2002.

Fox, Michael W. *Beyond Evolution: The Genetically Altered Future of Plants, Animals, the Earth, and Humans*. New York, NY: Lyon Press, 1999.

Grace, Eric S. *Biotechnology Unzipped: Promises and Realities*. Washington, DC: Joseph Henry Press, 1997.

Lurquin, Paul F. *High Tech Harvest: Understanding Genetically Modified Food Plants*. New York, NY: Westview Press, 2002.

Marshall, Elizabeth L. *High-Tech Harvest: A Look at Genetically Engineered Foods*. London, England: Franklin Watts, 1999.

McHughen, Alan. *Pandora's Picnic Basket: The Potential and Hazards of Genetically Modified Foods*. New York, NY: Oxford University Press, 2000.

Miller, Henry I. *The Frankenfood Myth: How Protest and Politics Threaten the Biotech Revolution*. Westport, CT: Praeger Publishers, 2004.

Pinstrup-Andersen, Per, and Ebbe Schioler. *Seeds of Contention: World Hunger and the Global Controversy Over GM (Genetically Modified) Crops*. Washington, DC: International Food Policy Research Institute, 2001.

Ruse, Michael. *Genetically Modified Foods: Debating Biotechnology* (Contemporary Issues Series). Amherst, NY: Prometheus Books, 2002.

Schlosser, Eric. *Fast Food Nation: The Dark Side of the All-American Meal.* New York, NY: Perennial, 2002.

Wiebe, Keith, Nicole Ballenger, Per Pinstrup-Andersen, and Keith Daniel Wiebe, eds. *Who Will Be Fed in the 21st Century?: Challenges for Science and Policy.* Washington, DC: International Food Policy Research Institute, 2001.

ANNOTATED BIBLIOGRAPHY

Alvarez, Lizette. "Consumers in Europe Resist Gene-Altered Foods." *New York Times*, February 11, 2003. Reporter Lizette Alvarez travels to England's West Country in this article to learn about British attitudes toward GM foods.
Copyright © 2003 by The New York Times Co. Reprinted with permission.

Bailey, Ronald. "Billions Served." *Reason*, Vol. 31, No. 11, April 2000. Bailey is the science correspondent for *Reason*, a monthly magazine on politics and culture. He is the author of *ECOSCAM: The False Prophets of Ecological Apocalypse* (1993) and editor of *Earth Report 2000: Revisiting the True State of the Planet* (1999).
Reprinted with permission. Copyright Reason *magazine, www.reason.com.*

Branford, Sue. "Argentina's Bitter Harvest." *New Scientist*, Vol. 182, No. 2443, April 17, 2004. In this article, Branford looks at a developing environmental crisis in Argentina blamed on the introduction of GM crops.
Reprinted with permission from New Scientist.

Brody, Jane E. "Facing Biotech Foods Without the Fear Factor." *New York Times*, January 11, 2005. Brody is a health columnist, science news reporter, and author of a number of cookbooks devoted to healthy eating, including *Jane Brody's Good Food Gourmet* (1990).
Copyright © 2005 by The New York Times Co. Reprinted with permission.

Charles, Daniel. *Lords of the Harvest: Biotech, Big Money, and the Future of Food.* Cambridge, MA: Perseus, 2001. Daniel Charles has been a technology correspondent for National Public Radio and a U.S. correspondent for *New Scientist*.
From LORDS OF THE HARVEST: BIOTECH, BIG MONEY, AND THE FUTURE OF FOOD by DANIEL CHARLES. Copyright 2001 by Daniel Charles. Reprinted by permission of Basic Books, a member of Perseus Books, L.L.C.

"Far Less Scary Than It Used to Be." *Economist*, Vol. 368, No. 8334, July 24, 2003, pp. 23–25. This article compares and contrasts the European perspective on GM foods to those of other countries, including the United States.
© 2003 The Economist Newspaper Ltd. All rights reserved. Reprinted with permission. Further reproduction prohibited. www.economist.com.

Fedoroff, Nina, and Nancy Marie Brown. *Mendel in the Kitchen: A Scientist's View of Genetically Modified Foods.* Washington, DC: Joseph Henry Press, 2004. Fedoroff is a professor at Penn State University specializing in plant genetics and molecular biology; Brown is a science writer with more than twenty years of writing experience.
Reprinted with permission from (Mendel in the Kitchen: A Scientist's View of Genetically Modified Foods) © (2004) by the National Academy of Sciences, courtesy of the National Academies Press, Washington, D.C.

Feffer, John. "The World in a Seed." AlterNet.org, September 25, 2004 (http://www.alternet.org/envirohealth/19998/). AlterNet.org is an online news site that provides free content to 1.5 million readers every month. The site is a project of the Independent Media Institute, a nonprofit organization dedicated to supporting independent and alternative journalism.
Reprinted with permission from John Feffer.

Fleeson, Lucinda. "A Cure for the Common Farm?" *Mother Jones*, Vol. 28, No. 2, March/April 2003, pp. 17–18. Fleeson is an award-winning journalist and the director of the Hubert H. Humphrey Fellowship Program in Journalism at the University of Maryland.
Reprinted with permission from Mother Jones. © 2003, Foundation for National Progress.

Hart, Kathleen. *Eating in the Dark: America's Experiment with Genetically Engineered Food.* New York, NY: Vintage, 2003. Hart has written about health and the environment for more than fifteen years. She has worked as a reporter for *Food Chemical News* and served as editor of the *Environmental Health Letter*.

From EATING IN THE DARK by Kathleen Hart, copyright © 2002, 2003 by Kathleen Hart. Used by permission of Pantheon Books, a division of Random House, Inc.

Jacobson, Michael F. "Agricultural Biotechnology: Savior or Scourge?" Center for Science in the Public Interest Web site. May 22, 2001 (http://www.cspinet.org/biotech/nab_conference.html). Jacobson is the executive director of the Center for Science in the Public Interest, an organization advocating, according to their Web site, "nutrition and health, food safety, alcohol policy, and sound science."

NATIONAL AGRICULTURAL BIOTECHNOLOGY CONFERENCE AGRICULTURAL BIOTECHNOL by JACOBSON, MICHAEL F. Copyright 2001 by CTR FOR SCI IN THE PUBLIC INTEREST. Reproduced with permission of CTR FOR SCI IN THE PUBLIC INTEREST in the format Other Book via Copyright Clearance Center.

Lambrecht, Bill. *Dinner at the New Gene Café: How Genetic Engineering Is Changing What We Eat, How We Live, and the Global Politics of Food*. New York, NY: St. Martin's Press, 2001. Lambrecht writes about the environment for the *St. Louis Post-Dispatch*. He has won three Raymond Clapper Awards for excellence in reporting.

From Dinner at the New Gene Café by Bill Lambrecht. Copyright © 2001 by the author and reprinted by permission of St. Martin's Press, LLC.

Nash, J. Madeleine. "Grains of Hope." *Time*, Vol. 156, No. 5, July 31, 2000. Nash specializes in science and technology for *Time* and has received three awards from the American Association for the Advancement of Science for excellence in science journalism.

© 2000 TIME Inc. reprinted by permission.

Pollan, Michael. *The Botany of Desire: A Plant's-Eye View of the World*. New York, NY: Random House, 2001. Pollan has won numerous awards for his writing, including the

Reuters/World Conservation Union Global Award in Environmental Journalism, the James Beard Award, and the Genesis Award from the American Humane Association.

From THE BOTANY OF DESIRE by Michael Pollan, copyright © 2001 by Michael Pollan. Used by permission of Random House, Inc.

Pringle, Peter. *Food, Inc.: Mendel to Monsanto—The Promises and Perils of the Biotech Harvest.* New York, NY: Simon & Schuster, 2003. Pringle is a British journalist who has worked as a staff correspondent for the *Sunday Times*, the *Observer*, and the *Independent*. He currently lives in New York City.

Reprinted with the permission of Simon & Schuster, Adult Publishing Group from FOOD, INC. by Peter Pringle. Copyright © 2003 by Peter Pringle.

Watson, James D., with Andrew Berry. *DNA: The Secret of Life.* New York, NY: Knopf, 2003. Watson, recipient of the 1962 Nobel Prize in Physiology or Medicine, is also the author of *The Double Helix* (1968), his account of the elucidation of the structure of DNA.

From DNA by James D. Watson and with Andrew Berry, copyright © 2003 by DNA Show LLC. Used by permission of Alfred A. Knopf, a division of Random House, Inc.

Winston, Mark L. *Travels in the Genetically Modified Zone.* Cambridge, MA: Harvard University Press, 2002. Winston is a professor of biology at Simon Fraser University in Vancouver, Canada. He is also the author of *Nature Wars: People Vs. Pests* (1997).

Reprinted by permission of the publisher from TRAVELS IN THE GENETICALLY MODIFIED ZONE by Mark L. Winston, pp. 13–18, 22–26, Cambridge, Mass.: Harvard University Press, Copyright © 2002 by the President and Fellows of Harvard College.

INDEX

A

Agrobacterium tumefasciens,
   28–31, 32–33, 99–100
Ames, Bruce, 51

B

Bacillus thuringiensis (Bt),
   37–39, 50, 77, 97, 100,
   106, 107, 108, 109, 114,
   116, 138, 161
   and Monarch butterflies,
      76, 162
   and StarLink corn, 130
Beachy, Roger, 39
Beyer, Peter, 68, 70, 74
Borlaug, Norman, 43, 44–51,
   58–60, 61
Boyer, Herbert, 21–24, 30,
   31, 119
Braun, Armin, 28
Bush, George, 122, 123, 124

C

Calgene, 40–41, 124
Capron, Horace, 54, 55
Carson, Rachel, 36
Carter, Jimmy, 72
Chang, Annie, 23
Chilton, Mary-Dell, 29, 30
chimera, 21, 24, 31, 95
China, 39, 167
Clinton, Bill, 49
Cohen, Stanley, 21–24, 30,
   31, 119
Conko, Gregory, 90

Conway, Gordon, 72
corporations
   AgrEvo, 138, 139–140
   Asgrow Seed Company, 124
   AstraZeneca, 74–75
   Aventis CropScience, 29, 131
   Calgene, 40–41, 124
   DeKalb, 137–142
   farmers dependent on, 20,
      33–34, 86–87, 102
   Garst Seeds, 19
   Pioneer Hi-Bred (Du Pont),
      18, 34, 138, 139, 141, 142
   and seed/gene ownership, 7,
      17, 85, 86, 96, 100,
      102–104, 137-143
   and Soviet Union, 34–35
   Syngenta, 163–164
Crick, Francis, 5, 21, 32
crop/seed selection, 12–15, 20
   and natural selection, 14–15

D

Darwin, Charles, 13, 14, 15
DDT, 36, 47
Dry, Lisa, 67
dwarf plants in Japan, 53–55, 58
dwarf wheat, 44, 55

E

Ehrlich, Paul, 44–45
Environmental Protection
      Agency (EPA), 37, 96,
      108–109, 117, 118, 119,
      122, 125, 126, 131, 133

environmentalists, 6, 43, 48, 53, 70, 97, 106
European colonization, 12
extinction, 81

F

Food and Drug Administration (FDA), 90, 109–111, 114, 117, 118, 119, 122, 124–128, 132, 133, 134, 136

G

Garst, Roswell, 9, 16–20, 34
genetic engineering
  definition of, 6
  Genetically Engineered Food Alert, 66, 131, 132, 133, 135
  genetic recombination, 13
  possible environmental benefits, 43, 106
GM crops,
  economic concerns and, 7, 149, 152–154, 158
  environmental dangers of, 6–7, 108, 148, 149–151
GM foods
  and allergies, 75, 108, 124, 131
  already in food supply, 7–8
  labeling of, 8, 88–89, 110–114, 122, 124, 125, 132, 134, 144, 147, 166
  and potential for toxins, 92, 127
  public understanding of, 90–91

golden rice, 42, 68–74, 80, 115
Gonsalves, Dennis, 78
Goodman, Howard, 23
Gordon, Milton, 29
Great Depression, 19
green revolution, 9, 43–45, 51, 55, 57, 58, 60, 62, 69, 73
Griffith, Fred, 28

H

Hawaiian papayas, 39, 78, 107
herbicides, 6–7, 35, 46, 49, 79, 107, 124, 138, 149, 150–156, 160
Holden, Ron, 137–141, 143
Horan, Bill, 63–66
Horsch, Rob, 5, 8, 30

I

India, 44–45, 58, 61, 62

K

Khrushchev, Nikita, 34
Kloppenberg, Jack, 57
Kraft, 131, 133, 135–136

L

Lederberg, Joshua, 24–25, 26
Losey, John, 76

M

MacArthur, Douglas, 54
Mellon, Margaret, 77
Mendel, Gregor, 9, 13, 14
  education of, 15
  and pea experiment, 15–16

Miller, Henry I., 90, 93
Monsanto Corporation, 5, 6, 7, 8,
   30, 39, 76, 93, 97, 98, 99,
   100, 103, 104, 105, 146,
   163–164, 167
   in Argentina, 150–158
   history of, 136, 138–143
   and responsibility for food
      safety, 128
   Roundup (Ready), 35, 46, 66,
      71, 124, 136–137, 138,
      143, 149, 152–158
Morel, Georges, 28
Morrow, John, 23

N

Nestor, Eugene, 29, 30
NewLeaf potatoes, 94,
   95–99, 101

O

organic farmers/farming, 37, 76

P

pesticides/insecticides, 7, 36–38,
   49, 76, 77, 86, 96, 97,
   108, 113, 119
   organic, 37, 116, 130
   and related illnesses, 37
pharmaceutical crops/
   pharmacrops, 63–67
Phytophthora infestans, 52
Pippin, Horace, 83
Potrykus, Ingo, 68–70,
   73–75, 80

Q

Quayle, Dan, 123–124

R

Reagan, Ronald, 118, 122
recombinant DNA
   (technology/techniques)
   "gene gun", 33, 99
   history of, 21–, 32–33,
      119–120
   homologous recombination, 25
   transduction, 26–27
Rhône-Poulenc, 124
Rockefeller Foundation, 42, 44,
   58, 59, 72, 73, 74, 79
Roosevelt, Franklin D., 18, 34, 57

S

Salmon, Cecil, 55
Sanford, John, 33
Schell, Jef, 29, 30
Schimke, Robert, 23
Shiyu, Leslie, 22
Stalin, Josef, 34
Starck, Dave, 99, 101
StarLink, 129, 130, 131, 132, 135
Swaminathan, M. S., 62

T

Tabashnik, Bruce, 77
Taco Bell, 131, 135
Toenniessen, Gary, 73

U

United States Department of Agriculture (USDA), 108, 115,
   117, 118, 119, 122, 125

V

Van Montagu, Marc, 29, 30
Veneman, Ann, 67

W

Wallace, Henry A., 18, 34
Wambugu, Florence, 78–79
Watson, James, 5, 21
  proponent of
    biotechnology, 32

Weaver, William Woys, 81–88
Wilkins, Maurice, 32
World Bank, 60

Z

Zinder, Norton, 24, 26

About the Editor

Susan Gordon is a writer and editor in New York City. Her life-long fascination with all kinds of food led to a professional culinary degree and a strong interest in the issues surrounding genetically modified foods. She currently works as a science and social science editor for a large educational publisher.

Credits

Cover, p. 1 © Andy Sacks/Getty Images.

Designer: Gene Mollica; Series Editor: Brian Belval
Photo Researcher: Gene Mollica